IMPROVING TRAINER EFFECTIVENESS

Improving Trainer Effectiveness

Edited by Roger Bennett

Gower

Published by
Gower Publishing Company Limited,
Gower House,
Croft Road,
Aldershot,
Hants GU11 3HR,
England

Gower Publishing Company,
Old Post Road,
Brookfield,
Vermont 05036,
USA

British Library Cataloguing in Publication Data

Improving trainer effectiveness.
   1. Employees, Training of
   I. Bennett, Roger
658.3'124   HF5549.5.T7

ISBN 0-566-02647-3

Printed in Great Britain at
the University Press, Cambridge

Contents

Notes on Contributors

Roger Bennett, BSc, MSc, PhD, MBIM, CENC–MIProdE., FITD, FRSA, ABPsS, is Professor of Management Education and Training at the International Management Centre from Buckingham and was formerly Head of Postgraduate Studies and Research at the Oxford School of Business, Oxford Polytechnic. After serving an engineering apprenticeship at Vickers Ltd, he gained substantial teaching, training, consulting and research experience at Portsmouth Polytechnic. He was then Reader in Management at the Thames Valley Regional Management Centre. He has worked with many major companies, has carried out research into trainer effectiveness for the UK's Manpower Services Commission, and has conducted numerous seminars and workshops on trainer effectiveness. Dr Bennett's numerous publications – journal papers and books – include many on trainer effectiveness. He is co-publisher of human resources journals at MCB, editor of the *Journal of European Industrial Training* and of *Business Education,* and was consultant editor and contributor to the Trainer Support Services (UK) project on developing workbooks for Training Managers.

Peter Bowen is Company Training Manager of W.H. Smith and Son Limited with executive responsibility for management training and development. His professional interests are in the performance development of managers by training, and in open learning. Previously he was Director of the Centre of Employment Policy Studies at Henley, the Management College, and Head of the Department of Behavioural Studies at Newcastle Polytechnic.

Mr Bowen is a member of the CBI Education and Training Committee, is a CBI representative on the MSC's Open Tech Steering Group, and Chairman of the MSC's Quality Issues Sub-Committee. He lectures and consults internationally on management training and development and is an Associate Fellow of Templeton College, Oxford, a Visiting Fellow of Henley, the Management College, and Chairman of the Management Committee of the Oxford Consortium.

John Burgoyne, BSc, MPhil, PhD, is Professor in the Department in the Centre for the Study of Management Learning at Lancaster University. He was previously Research Director in CSML and Lecturer in Management Development at Manchester Business School. He has published, researched and consulted widely on managerial behaviour, evaluation of management development, management development policy, self-development approaches to management development, the nature of the learning process, and career management.

Julia Davies worked for British Rail and later the health service before moving to the Manchester Business School to research into management training provision for ward sisters. She now lectures in the Department of Management Learning at Lancaster University. Her work has included research and consultancy in the areas of: selection and development of trainers; evaluation of management development; links between organizational culture and the strategies of management development. Her publications include articles for a range of journals, including *Personnel Review* and *Journal of Management Studies,* and a book on management training in the organizational context of hospitals.

David Flegg, BSc, ABPS, and *Josephine McHale,* BA, MPhil, of the Hamelin Partnership, are consultant Occupational Psychologists. Both began their careers in other fields – David as an electrical engineer and Josephine in teaching – before taking degrees in psychology and specializing in its application to people at work. They worked at the Industrial Training Research Unit for several years before setting up their own business. Within the areas of training, development and selection, they take on many different roles: as direct trainers, as courseware writers and designers, as advisors and as developers of new approaches to selection and training. Through their research and their own practical experience, they have developed a particular interest in the training of trainers and in helping people learn.

Alun Jones, PhD, is currently Director – Research and Development of Industrial Training Services Ltd, an international consultancy service. Dr Jones has been mainly concerned with improving the effectiveness of training within organizations, in three principal areas:

Evaluation of Training: A fifteen-year research programme linked with university departments has developed evaluation and cost benefit analytical techniques which have been widely applied to training investments and practices.

Training of Trainers: Dr Jones was a member of the Training of Trainers' committee set up by the Manpower Services Commission in the UK. Subsequently he was a member of the MSC Training Advisory Group. He has advised and assisted in the development of trainers and consultants for the Civil Service and the National Health Service, as well as for multi-national private companies.

Organizational Learning and Development: Dr Jones' own main area of consultancy has been in helping organizations to cope with change and to learn how to learn as corporate entities. He has been in particular demand in helping top-management teams develop their own effectiveness.

Tad Leduchowicz is Deputy Director, Open Learning, at the Management Centre, Slough College. Since March 1985 he has been working on attachment to the Trainer Support Services (part of the Institute of Training and Development) as Development Manager, concerned with the development of open learning materials for Training Managers and Senior Managers and has been involved with helping occasional trainers in the Electricity Supply Industry.

His recent activities have included research work on trainer effectiveness and the use of training packages in a number of large organizations, including Hewlett Packard, Rank Xerox and British Caledonian.

Tad gained a Masters Degree in Education, after being educated as a biologist. He has worked at the Institute of Child

Health in London, taught biology at Boreham Wood College of Further Education, and was a researcher at Thames Valley Regional Management Centre.

Charles Margerison, BSc, DIA, CDipAF, PhD, is Professor of Management and Director of the Management Education Research Unit at the University of Queensland, Australia. He has substantial management training and consulting experience around the world, is a prolific author (including seven books) and is vice president of the International Management Centre from Buckingham. Previous academic appointments were at Bradford and Cranfield Business Schools, prior to which he worked in manufacturing and local government. He is co-publisher of human resource journals at MCB and is editor/founding editor of the *Journal of Management Development, Journal of Managerial Psychology,* and *Managerial Auditing Journal.*

Howard Silverfarb has over 20 years of international experience in Human Resource Development, has held executive positions in multinational firms in Asia, the US, Europe and Africa, and has considerable experience in management and executive training and development. As ASEAN Regional Director of Training and Development for Banque Nationale de Paris in Singapore, he has achieved wide exposure to the training scene in South East Asia. Previously he was BNP's North East Asia's Director of Training based in Hong Kong, and has been in training in Africa, the US and Spain. He is currently Associate Consultant with Roger Gill and Associates in Singapore.

Phillip Wright, PhD, is Assistant Professor of Human Resources Development at the Canadian School of Management, Teaching Master in the Business Division of Humber College, National Education Co-ordinator for the Canadian Institute of Management and Member of the UK's Institute of Training and Development. He has published widely on a variety of management topics in Canada, Britain and the United States and acts as a consultant, specializing in the design and delivery of learning programmes.

Preface

'The road to success is always under construction.'

Training is a frustrating business. Just when we've got one good programme or event under way, tried and tested to the satisfaction of most people, changes occur that force us to reconstruct, or even demolish and rebuild, what we are doing. Take the example of one training manager who, after eight years of dedicated, patient and rigorous development of a highly job-related, effective management development workshop series, found that his new senior management did not want this approach. He had to start building all over again. But such changes do occur and have to be tackled. We also have to face up to other issues and obstacles on the road to success.

- *Some people* hold perverse views about training. They believe it to be necessary, yet doubt its value and relevance.

- *Some trainers* also hold perverse views about training. They believe what they do is right, yet are not committed to organizational success.

  BUT

- *All trainers* can be successful i.e. do the right things and do them well. *They can* integrate what they do with the real needs of their organizations.

- *This book* will help you to achieve that important goal. Each chapter is geared to *helping you* to get on the road to success and to maintain that success.

- *Your effort* in working through the exercises and checklists will ensure that you gain that success – the success that you and all trainers deserve. Without successful trainers, the future will be bleak, and the roadworks unending.

HOW THIS BOOK CAN HELP YOU

This book has been designed to help you improve your effectiveness at both a) doing your current job and b) adapting to change. It is not a conventional book. Contributors have been drawn from across the world and are known for their excellence. Their contributions are aimed at helping you to *understand* more fully what is involved in being effective and in *doing* things to work through issues and to take *action*. There are checklists, review questions and other devices designed to set you thinking and acting constructively.

We start the process in Chapter 1 by looking at what we mean by trainer effectiveness and placing it in the context of key changes that will affect what we do as trainers.

In Chapter 2 we identify the factors that influence trainer effectiveness, with many exercises aimed at getting you to do this with respect to your own job and situation. Chapter 3 looks at the different jobs or roles trainers perform, how to develop your job/role and how to gain influence through your job/role. We then move on to consider how trainers can become more effective as instructors, change agents and management developers (Chapters 4, 5 and 6). But your effectiveness depends on having a good training policy, sound management of the training function, a full understanding of careers for trainers and of the culture with which training must work. These are taken up in Chapters 7, 8, 9 and 10. We conclude by looking at some of the factors that make for excellence in helping the organization to be a success. We all hope very much that you will find this book both stimulating and helpful – more of a workbook than a textbook – and wish you every success in your job.

Roger Bennett

Acknowledgements

This book has come about through the contributions, both direct and indirect, of very many people. As Editor, I owe all these people sincere thanks for their contributions.

The main direct contributors are the authors of the individual chapters. I would like to acknowledge their willingness and keenness to become involved in this venture and to thank them for the hard work and effort they have put into preparing their material.

Some of this material has drawn, in part, upon studies and projects funded by the UK's Manpower Services Commission. We acknowledge the source and thank MSC for permission to draw upon it. Through those studies and projects, many people have contributed in an indirect way to the development of this book. We would also like to acknowledge their efforts.

I should also like to thank John Zenger, Trainer Support Services, and the Institute of Training and Development for giving permission to draw upon and quote from various sources and materials. Acknowledgements are also due to those practitioners, writers and researchers upon whose work we have drawn in the conventional way with appropriate acknowledgements being made in the references and notes.

A book comes into shape only when written materials have been typed, checked through and put into print. I should like to thank the various secretaries of the contributors to the book, and my own secretary Christine Bloore, for their patient help in translating our thinking and ideas into a readable format. Sincere

xiv   **IMPROVING TRAINER EFFECTIVENESS**

thanks also go to Malcolm Stern and his colleagues at Gower for their dedicated work in helping to see this book through to its final stages.

Finally, I would wish to thank you, the reader, for being prepared to pick up this book and read it. I hope you will gain stimulation from doing so.

Whilst acknowledging the efforts of all those people who have contributed to the book, as Editor I must accept final responsibility for what you are about to read. I trust, on behalf of all my colleagues, that you will find the book of interest and practical use.

R.B.

1 What Is Trainer Effectiveness?

Roger Bennett

This book is about how to improve trainer effectiveness. It offers practical guidance and ways of thinking about the work of trainers that will lead to better performance. It makes the assumption that trainers are still an important part of any organizational or economic activity. Although it may seem to you (and to others) that this assumption is sometimes stretched in today's world economic, financial and political climate, it is still the case that trainers are much needed people.

Far apart geographically the UK and Singapore may be, they are fairly close in their need for trainers. The UK has, indeed, closed some of its Industrial Training Boards, but it is pouring massive amounts of money into vocational and youth training. In Singapore, it has been recognized that increased skills are needed to sustain or improve national performance and move away from a low-wage economy. Through its Skill Development Fund, it is working well to achieve this. In both countries, effective trainers are needed to achieve government's objectives. This is true across the world.

It is also true in specific industries and companies. Trainers are still in demand, because training is needed and is vital to success. From studies of successful companies in the UK and USA we know that, among a relatively small number of factors (up to about eight), training plays its part. Successful companies stress training, both as a way of increasing efficiency and as a means of instilling the company's values into employees. Although many such employees may not be exceptional, the successful companies get from them extraordinary levels of performance. They do this not only through training the employees but also by developing the managers to provide exceptional leadership. They also spend a lot of money on training – but so do some unsuccessful companies. The difference is that successful companies make sure that training is effective – that it is related to its future needs in a consistent and planned way. It is business oriented.

But the way trainers make a successful contribution to their company's performance – and the nature of that contribution –has changed. This change has come about because circumstances have changed, and successful trainers have changed, too. In this book we want to point out some ways in which you can change, adapt and grow with your organization, and get some real enjoyment from your work. But first, we need to look at the meaning and nature of trainer effectiveness and relate this to the changing circumstances in which you have to operate.

WHAT IS 'TRAINER EFFECTIVENESS'?

To answer this question, we must first look at the meaning of the word 'effectiveness'. Effectiveness is concerned with achieving goals, targets, or results. To be 'effective' is to do the job you are actually supposed to do, to get the results expected of you.

As a term, or concept, effectiveness is often confused with efficiency. Indeed, it is not uncommon to hear both terms used to describe the same idea. This is wrong. Efficiency means getting the most out of the resources – all resources – you have at your disposal. It is a measure of input to output. Effectiveness is about ensuring the output is the one you really wanted or intended.

Being effective implies some degree of efficiency. However, efficiency need not imply effectiveness. We can be efficient at achieving irrelevant goals or objectives.

The two can best be summarized using the words of the inimitable Peter Drucker:

effectiveness is doing the right things,
efficiency is doing things right.

To be effective as a trainer you must continually ask yourself 'what am I here for?'. You may be tempted to answer, 'to train people'. This is, or may be, undoubtedly true, except that you do not train people simply for the sake of it. You do so because there is a need for training, derived from organizational needs. Overall, training is used to improve performance, or at least contribute to improving the performance of the organization. This we would call 'overall effectiveness'. It is the relationship between the correct identification of organizational needs, the selection of those needs that can be satisfied through training, the translation of these into training objectives, engaging in training activities that are in line with the organization's culture and achieving outcomes that contribute to the organization's goals.

This level of effectiveness is not easy to measure. Other things, such as methods of working, managerial ability, market conditions and so on, will also contribute to the achievement of the organization's goals. If, however, training is 'business oriented' i.e. linked clearly to the operational and development needs of the organization, then effectiveness can be achieved. Some trainers find it helpful to 'talk the language' of senior management when discussing the role and contribution of training. They seek to demonstrate that training will help improve profits, sell more products or improve the services offered. If this can be done in financial or quantitative terms, so much the better. So, your main, overall objective is to contribute to the organization's success.

You do this by providing various training activities that satisfy particular organizational needs. Your organization may be introducing microcomputers to speed up the handling of customer orders and invoicing. Few employees have the skill required to operate the equipment, and you have found it difficult to recruit trained personnel. You know how many you have to train and by when. The training involves understanding what micros are all about and giving practical experience in using them. Your goal is, therefore, quite clear. You can also 'measure' the extent to which you have achieved it by giving practical tests to the employees. This we call 'interim effectiveness'. There will be many such specific training activities with which you will be involved. Each one must work, must pay off. Thus, interim effectiveness concerns the achievement of the many intermediate, shorter-term goals that are part of your job – part of the 'what are you here for'. They can be as specific as researching the subject matter of the training activity, preparing relevant handouts or checklists, or selling your services to the rest of the organization. But, they must all be linked to the main purpose of contributing to the organization's success. If they are not, your excellent training will have little or no longer-term impact on the organization.

Remember:

- always ask 'what am I here for'
- make sure you know and understand the business needs of your organization
- base your training on those needs
- talk in the language of senior management
- don't confuse effectiveness with efficiency
- lots of activity doesn't mean you are being effective.

WHAT IS THE NATURE OF THE TRAINER'S WORK?

Typically, trainers are seen as people who instruct others in the ways in which a job, activity, process or operation should be carried out. They do this in training rooms (classrooms, lecture rooms), in laboratories, in workshops or in other places specifically designed for the purpose of 'instruction'. This will be with a wide range of employees – from operators and clerks through supervisors to managers. The significant part of the work is imparting knowledge and developing skills and attitudes. This is certainly a view of the trainer's work that probably held true in the past. According to one study, about half of the people taking part in a questionnaire survey had job titles that suggested this is still so, at least in the UK. The same survey showed that nearly half of the sample were engaged in instruction or teaching as a large part of their jobs. In the same study, but with a different sample and using interviews instead of a questionnaire, the proportion involved in 'direct training' was 67 per cent. It is clear, therefore, that instructing, teaching or direct training is still a very important part of the trainer's work.

There are, however, many other activities that trainers undertake. They include all those things that make the training possible (such as preparation, planning, administration) and other activities that are either complementary to direct training (e.g. advising, coaching) or represent a difference in approach (e.g. organization development). The following list describes activities obtained from interviews with over 100 trainers.

	%
Direct Training – Face-to-face contact with groups of trainees – tutoring, instruction, teaching, seminars, workshops	67
Planning and Preparation – Course development, planning, preparation, background research	62
Need Identification and Analysis – Identifying needs, analysis, diagnosis, setting training objectives, preparation of training plans, determining future needs	60
Involvement in Educational Technology – Preparation of AV materials, learning materials, training packages	38
Keeping Informed – Monitoring what goes on, researching, conducting surveys, acting as information provider, updating course material	33
Administration – Course bookings, etc.	33
Management – Managing the training functions and training staff	29
Interacting with Individuals – Counselling, coaching	27
Evaluation – Evaluation of training programmes	27
Contact with Outside Agencies – Developing contacts, visiting establishments, organizing external courses, dealing with day release, liaison with educational establishments, dealing with ITBs, getting outside consultants to give presentations	27
Advising – Advising people in the organization	24
Development Activities – Non-course development activities – action groups, 'think-tanks', OD activities	22
Meetings – Attending meetings, committee work	18
Financial Aspects of Training – Costing training and getting approval, resourcing activities	18
Liaison – Liaison with personnel function and others in the organization	18

The main focus or features of the trainer's work will depend upon the needs of the organization and what managers expect the trainer to do. Both the needs and expectations are changing, because the context or situation in which many organizations operate are changing.

THE CHANGING CONTEXT OF THE TRAINER'S WORK

There is little doubt that fundamental change is affecting many organizations across the world. Although change is something we have faced for decades, the rate, pace and scope of change currently are quite massive. The changes cover almost the entire spectrum of economic, political, social and technological aspects of our environment. Here we shall look at some of these and consider their implications for trainers.

Economic change

It is fair to say that most countries have serious economic problems. The turn-down in the world economy, the problems with exchange rates and the uncertainty in the oil markets have caused severe difficulties for many organizations. The pressure to make companies leaner and fitter in a harsh competitive world is real. This is felt through the increased unit costs in many countries. For example, the OECD estimated that, in the mid 1980s, the increased unit costs in certain countries were as follows:

UK	6%
France	5%
Italy	4%
US	2.2%

For others, there was a reduction:

Japan	−0.2%
Canada	−0.5%
West Germany	−1%
Netherlands	−2%

Reducing unit costs requires an increase in output for the same resource or the same output with fewer resources. This can be achieved in many ways, but often training has to be geared to meet specific unit cost requirements. And training itself is now often judged on the same basis – is it cost effective?

Trainers are expected not only to help the organization achieve better unit costs (e.g. through providing people who can tackle many skills or jobs) but also to do so as cheaply as possible. This means that trainers must look to the methods they use to train people. In some cases, this has resulted in fewer off-the-job training activities and more on-the-job development, including helping managers and supervisors to become skilled at training and coaching.

Technological change

We see this occurring more and more each year. The important advances in the use, for example, of robotics and information technology have transformed many factories and offices. Many tasks can now be performed at the touch of a button. But behind that button lies a whole new range of expertise. Robots have to be programmed, and computers control complete production systems turning out a mix of products. Highly skilled programmers and technicians are required. This means that trainers have to be knowledgeable of the new technology. In the information technology field, the skills of, say, the typist are still required, plus many more. Learning the codes and instructions to operate a wordprocessor is no easy matter. Engineers now frequently have their own desk top computers – and not many have previously had to work with computers at all. They will look to the trainer for help.

If technological change still has not caught up with you, it will in the future. Just consider the following points:

- one robot can produce what six car workers used to;
- the fifth generation of computers is already here, yet the fourth generation has only just been introduced;
- by 1999, 70 per cent of the types of work would not have existed 25 years earlier, and
- by the year 2000, 80 per cent of our pets will be electronic! (according to one US expert interviewed on British radio in 1985).

The ability to design and produce smaller yet more powerful equipment, to manufacture goods without (many) people, to send mail without letters or envelopes, to hold conferences without meeting . . . . . is here. Trainers must help their organizations make use of that ability – and they must make use of it themselves. Video, computer-based training and the like must become part of the trainer's technology, too. For many who are apprehensive of this ability, change will not be easy. To survive, and be effective, trainers must change.

Social and political change

Change in the social and political environment is, perhaps the most difficult to come to terms with and do anything about. Often, it is bound up with economic and technological change, and with the stance of national government. Unemployment is a good example. Most governments do not want it, yet can do little about it. Where they try, they must make choices. Do they encourage investment in the future (by training the young, as many Western European countries have emphasized) or do they provide training help for those who are unemployed (which requires special counselling skills of a high order from trainers)? Many find that the economic situation will not allow them to do both. Switches in government policy from one to another emphasis can leave many trainers with redundant skills and experience. Policies for encouraging self-employment and small businesses make further demands on the skill and experience of trainers. Some will have to specialize, and then retrain themselves. For the individual trainer in a particular organization, such concerns may seem to warrant little attention. Yet for the organization itself, social and political change may have far reaching effects. It is the *duty* of trainers to make sure they are aware of such changes and can adapt to them, and help the organization cope with them.

In addition, many countries face the social and political issue of equal rights and opportunities for specific groups. These may include women returning to work, the disabled, and ethnic and religious groups. All of these impose cultural constraints on what the trainer can and should do. Such constraints may be set out in the laws passed by the government. Trainers will not only have to understand these constraints (or requirements) but also be able to adopt appropriate training methods, styles and languages in order to cope with them.

Areas of change affecting the trainer

All of these sources of change point to four key areas that trainers must think about and be prepared to respond to. They have to be concerned with:

- knowledge change area: understanding the general cognitive or conceptual implications;
- skill change area: incorporating new ways of performing to help the organization be successful;

- attitude change area: adapting new feelings by experiencing success with them, and
- values change area: rearranging old beliefs and adopting new ones in line with changes in the culture of the organization and its environment.

This means that, to be effective, trainers must confront the changing reality and change with it. Not to do so will end in extinction, as many have found to their cost.

Helping the organization to change

As we shall make clear a little later on, parts of this book are designed to help trainers to change, and to help them help their organizations to change. At this stage, having pointed out some of the pressures for change and summarized the main change areas, we wish to highlight some of the general requirements for helping change to come about. This is based on the assumption that most organizations and trainers will face the need to adapt to new circumstances and is therefore important in improving the effectiveness of the contribution trainers can make to organizational success. We also assume that change is not an everlasting phenomenon and will later discuss ways of improving effectiveness in non-change circumstances.

Most authorities recognize that there has to exist a *climate for change* – both general and specific. Some of the conditions or characteristics of such climates include:

- being 'invaded' by liberal, creative and unconventional outsiders with fresh views and ideas;
- these outsiders are exposed to creative, competent and flexible internal agents who can help them adapt (i.e. become 'socialized');
- staffed by young, flexible, supportive and competent managers who operate across departmental boundaries;
- structurally complex and decentralized organization;
- outside funds to provide 'organizational slack' necessary for low cost innovation;
- protection of members' status by effects of change, and
- is located in modern, urban settings with other organizations that can supplement its skills and resources, and not bound by hard tradition.

You might fruitfully use these points as a checklist for the change potential of your organization.

A second important requirement is for *diagnosis and action*. This involves working through the following steps:

- sensing that there is a problem, or a need for change;
- defining the nature of the problem or need;
- generating alternatives for action or solutions;
- evaluating and assessing the alternatives;
- creating a plan of action;
- implementing the plan of action;
- evaluating the outcomes of the action, and
- taking further action decisions as necessary.

This process, well-known to Organization Development specialists, is one that many trainers find useful in getting close to the real needs of the organization and in establishing the role training can play in helping to cope with change. It is also one that trainers can develop successful workshops around for developing managers' skills in handling the change process.

Operating the change process depends on knowing what to do and when to do certain things. Some of the practical issues here include:

- understanding that there is a range of 'buttons' (or triggers) that can be pressed and knowing what those buttons are;
- determining which buttons to press, where and when;
- appreciating when a particular change button has been pressed for too long a period in a particular set of circumstances, and
- identifying which people among trainers or other HRD specialists have the capacity and skills to push buttons and ensuring that they are dispersed around the organization to facilitate change.

The nature of the 'buttons' will vary. They may include, for example, a crisis, a powerful manager, a change in policy, a change in top management, and so on. Do you know which buttons exist, and how to push them?

We can conclude by stating that trainers face a changing environment, potential major change in the organization, pressures to adopt new ways of working and a need to become involved in helping the organization to adapt to change successfully.

REVIEW QUESTIONS

In preparation for working through the rest of this book, we invite you to ask yourself the following questions, and to answer them fully and honestly. You may find it helpful to do this yourself, and then work through them with some colleagues. This could be the start of an important development exercise for the training function.

1   What are the attitudes of managers in your organization to the training function?
2   What expectations do senior managers have of the training function?
3   Is the training you provide really linked to the key needs of your organization?
4   Have you any means of judging the effectiveness of your contributions to the organization?
5   Can you adequately answer the question 'what am I here for'?
6   Can you state the range of activities you carry out?
7   Do you know which are the really important ones?
8   Can you state the nature of changes the organization is facing and in what areas they are occurring?
9   Can you operate in such a way as to help the organization adapt to change?
10   Do you have the skill, experience and support to cope with change yourself and to improve your effectiveness?

You can find answers to these, and many related questions, by working through this book.

REMEMBER, THERE ARE NO 'CORRECT' ANSWERS – ONLY ONES THAT ARE APPROPRIATE TO YOUR SITUATION.

SUGGESTED FURTHER READING

Some of the thoughts and concerns expressed in this chapter have been triggered by the studies and writings of other people. You may want to pursue some of them through further reading.

On trainer effectiveness

We have drawn on the work carried out for and funded by the UK's Manpower Services Commission. This was a study of the things that influenced trainer effectiveness. The findings can be found in:

Bennett, R. and Leduchowicz, T., 'What Makes for an Effective Trainer?', *Journal of European Industrial Training Monograph*, 1983, vol. 7, no. 2.

The work of others will also be of interest. See, for example:

McKay, L. and Torrington, D., 'Training in the UK – Down But Not Out?', *Journal of European Industrial Training*, 1986, vol. 10, no. 1, which reports on some aspects of a study of UK personnel directors.

On organizational effectiveness

There are many books and other sources that cover this issue. Some of the more readable ones are:

Goldsmith, W. and Clutterbuck, D., *The Winning Streak*, Weidenfeld and Nicholson, London, 1984.
Peters, T. and Waterman, R., *In Search of Excellence*, Harper & Row, New York, 1982.

These are based on studies of successful organizations in the UK and the USA (respectively).

On change

Some of the notable academic writings on this topic include:

Corwin, R., 'Strategies for Organisational Intervention – An Empirical Comparison', *American Sociological Review*, 1972, August, pp. 441–442.

Kast, F. and Rosenzweig, J. *Organisation and Management – A Systems Approach*, McGraw-Hill, New York, 1974.

Lippitt, G., *Organisation Renewal*, Prentice-Hall Inc., Englewood Cliffs, New Jersey, 1982.

Pettigrew, A., 'Sharing in the Human Resource Management Task – Roles for Personnel, Trainers and Managers?', *Proceedings of the National Conference of the Institute of Personnel Management*, UK, 1982.

These cover approaches to change, conditions and climates for change, the process of change, and 'what buttons to press' (Pettigrew) to achieve change, among other things. The first three are quite heavy reading in places, but contain very useful material.

2 The Key Factors

Tad Leduchowicz

Training plays an important part in the development of knowledge and skill in all sectors of the economies around the world. Just as the successful sportsperson must train to keep on winning, so too must any organization. Whilst the effectiveness of the sportsperson's coach is reflected by success in winning events, it is often more difficult to evaluate the success or effectiveness of the organizational trainer. Many other factors come into play in determining individual and organizational performance – methods of work used; efficient supply of materials; adequate equipment; attitudes of senior management, and of customers; the whims of the market place, government policy and the world economic situation. With so many variables involved it may seem futile to bother to study trainer effectiveness!

Recognizing many of the difficulties, an attempt* was made to do just this. The research was exploratory in nature and involved an interviewing programme with trainers and managers, questionnaires and a literature review. In the interviews the following areas were covered:

- organizational details;
- what the trainers do;
- what problems and constraints they encounter;
- what methods they use to cope with problems and constraints;

---

*A study carried out for the Manpower Services Commission (see Further Reading and References in Chapter 1 and at the end of this chapter).

- their views on trainer role and the criteria they would use to judge trainer effectiveness.

Extensive data were collected as a result of the research study and this led to the firm conclusion that there is no simple definition of trainer effectiveness. A model of trainer effectiveness which takes account of a broad range of factors is closer to the mark.

The research indicated that there are a number of key questions that can be used to examine trainer effectiveness. These are:

A. How do trainers see their role and responsibilities?

B On what activities do trainers spend their time?

C. What approaches do trainers adopt in their activities?

D. What knowledge and skills do trainers have?

E. What characteristics do trainers have?

F. What are the outcomes of trainers' activities?

G. How does the organization influence trainers?

REVIEWS

This chapter looks briefly at each of the above questions, and at the end of each section provides you with an opportunity to review your own situation. This will help you to identify positive and negative factors that influence your effectiveness as a trainer. Some of these factors are highlighted in the chapter: others will occur to you as you go through the review process.

Having identified positive and negative factors influencing your effectiveness you will be in a better position to build on the positive factors and to start tackling the negative factors.

A.   How do trainers see their role and responsibilities?

Role refers to the collection of behaviours, attitudes and values that are expected of a person occupying a given position in an organization or society. The expectations associated with some roles are clear, while those associated with other roles are less clear. Training falls into this latter category.

It has been said by Nadler (1969) that:

... there can be no single statement of what the role of a training specialist should be. It is conditioned by a combination of the objective necessities in his firm, subjective and personal elements brought out by the activities of managers, and his own conception of his role and personal skills – he and the job help to make each other.

The trainers' conception of their role is a critical element in determining their effectiveness in the organization. It is influenced by the trainer's own experience, qualities and skills and perception of what is expected of a trainer by senior staff.

While it is not possible to place trainers into watertight categories it is true to say that trainers have a recognizable orientation to their work. That is, there tends to be a consistency in the way trainers see and approach their work. Some see themselves as having a role to play in ensuring that existing systems are operating smoothly. Their orientation is primarily a maintenance one. They adopt a 'fire-fighting' approach to training by responding to problems and needs as they arise.

Other trainers see themselves as having a role to play in helping to bring about change in the organization. They adopt an interventionist approach. They anticipate future organizational needs and attempt to prepare people for change.

Trainers' reaction to change will determine the type of organizational needs they feel inclined to tackle and the importance they attach to different activities.

Another important factor is on what trainers model their activities. Some see training as being very similar in nature to the traditional educational process and model their activities on this. They see their role as the setting up of suitable courses that achieve a set training objective – they become 'experts' on the subject matter and convey their expertise to learners. Other trainers adopt a different stance. They see it as their responsibility to determine what the organizational needs are, to diagnose these and determine which can be tackled by a range of interventions that will bring about learning. These are not restricted to accepted or tried approaches, but incorporate many 'one-off' initiatives. We shall explore this in more detail in Chapter 3.

Having said this, it may be that the trainers' conception of their role has little real influence. There may be a clear role laid down for them by the Training Manager or by other managers. The training role may be a specialized one with the boundaries clearly defined or it may be very broad with a significant degree of flexibility. The trainer's position in the training 'hierarchy' is also important.

It may help to think of trainers as falling into four categories:

LEARNING STRATEGISTS – These are people who need a sufficiently good overview of the organization to be able to recognize key issues and problems and to determine those that have learning implications. They are responsible for giving direction to the training function, providing resources and monitoring the outcomes of training activity. They may also be involved in formulating a training policy for the organization and representing the training function at board level.

MANAGERS OF THE LEARNING FUNCTION – Essentially their role is that of any other manager i.e. making sure that the resources under their control are used to best effect.

LEARNING TECHNOLOGISTS – These are the trainers who are responsible for training design, preparation and implementation. Their methods of providing learning opportunities are diverse – they may have face-to-face contact with learners or act in a more remote way.

LEARNING ADMINISTRATORS – Their role is not so much concerned with training, but with supporting the training function. They could be administrators in any function in the organization.

How specialized the training role is will be determined by a whole range of factors, not least of all the size of the organization. In many smaller organizations, trainers may be responsible for carrying out the full range of roles. In larger organizations employing perhaps a number of trainers the role will be more specialized and probably more clearly defined.

The review that follows provides an opportunity to look at your role in general. In Chapter 3 we do this in detail.

REVIEW	A. ROLE AND RESPONSIBILITIES

How is your role determined?

Who do you report to?

To what extent does he or she (they?) influence what you do?

How in turn is he or she (they?) influenced?

Do you have a written job description? If yes, how does it relate to what you actually do?

Who generally takes the initiative in deciding what training will be done?

Do you prefer to get involved in 'maintenance' or 'change' activities? How does this fit in with organizational needs?

Do you tend to model your activities on educational processes or more on intervention? How does this fit in with organizational needs?

FACTORS INFLUENCING YOUR EFFECTIVENESS

Positive	*Negative*
e.g. able to adapt role to organizational needs	e.g. no links with people who have influence in the organization.
1	1
2	2
3	3

Taking positive action

Are you aware of the range of trainer roles? If not take steps to find out. Work carefully through Chapter 3.

Do you adopt a flexible role? Some roles will be more appropriate to particular organizational needs.

Has the organization 'locked' you into a particular role, or have you 'locked' yourself into a role? Take steps to break out!

B.   On what activities do you spend your time?

Efficiency is about doing things right. Effectiveness is about doing the right things. Potentially, in most organizations there are many needs that trainers could be called upon to respond to. However, a few needs will stand out as the critical ones. That is, satisfaction of them will produce significant benefits to the organization. Unless trainers are able to identify these and devote significant effort to dealing with them, they will not be effective. We can call these 'key effectiveness areas'.

The generalization is frequently made that twenty per cent of the problems solved can generate eighty per cent of the benefits. Effective trainers are those who are able to narrow down the needs to those which will produce most of the benefits and devote most of their time to satisfying them. There are, however, various reasons or pressures on the trainer to divert attention from dealing with the key areas:

- managers expect trainers to respond to *their* particular problems and needs irrespective of the priority that should be attributed to the needs;
- trainers get locked into dealing with certain needs or problems simply because of inertia or tradition;
- there is no regular review of organizational needs;
- managers do not convey to trainers information about needs as they see them;
- trainers have a preference for particular activities and may get involved in these irrespective of whether there is a demand or not, and
- the solutions to some needs or problems are easier to achieve so they are tackled in preference to more difficult needs or problems.

REVIEW	B. UTILIZATION OF TIME

What are the key issues in your organization?

To be effective as a trainer you must be able to distinguish which organizational needs you should be tackling – some will be more important than others. These will determine your 'key effectiveness areas'.

In order to determine your 'key effectiveness areas' you need first to consider where the organization is heading and what obstacles exist. A list of some possible organizational issues is given below. Tick any that you feel are important in your organization and indicate the level of importance by using the scale 1 (low importance) to 10 (high importance). Add any organizational issues that you feel are missing and rate their importance as before.

(i)   *What are the KEY ISSUES in your organization?*

Issue   *Level of importance*

                                                  (1 low–10 high)

Product or service issues:

Need to increase product or service quality   _____
Need to increase output   _____
Diversification of product or service range   _____
Rationalizing product or service range   _____
Moving into new markets   _____
Policy for development of existing and new
products   _____
Others:
....   _____
....   _____
....   _____

Financial issues

Need to increase profitability   _____
Reduction in cost of overheads   _____
Inadequate financial information   _____
Inability to finance growth   _____
Revision of pricing structures   _____
Others:
....   _____
....   _____
....   _____

Level of importance

Manpower issues: (1 low – 10 high)

Meeting manpower needs   _____
Reducing manpower levels   _____
Developing new skills   _____
Building greater job deployment flexibility   _____
Improving job performance   _____
Improving communication   _____
Improving group working   _____
Reduction of labour turnover   _____
Reduction of absenteeism   _____
Reduction of accidents   _____
Others:
....   _____
....   _____
....   _____

Equipment and materials issues:

Reducing waste   _____
Improving stock control   _____
Replacing obsolete equipment   _____
Introducing new technology   _____
Utilization of space   _____
Obsolete stocks   _____
Commissioning of new equipment   _____
Reduction of damage done to equipment   _____
Others:
....   _____
....   _____
....   _____

Other issues:

Health and safety regulations   _____
Need to reorganize departments   _____
Opening of new branches   _____
Others:
....   _____
....   _____
....   _____

(ii) *Shortlisting PRIORITY ISSUES*

List below the five organizational issues that you have rated as having the highest importance:

1 _____

2 _____

3 _____

4 _____

5 _____

(iii) *Identifying your 'key effectiveness areas'*

The next step is to decide if issues 1–5 can be resolved or partially resolved through training. The question you need to ask yourself is:

Does a lack of knowledge, lack of skills or inappropriate attitude in the workforce hinder the resolution of the particular issue?

If it does not then the solution is not a training one. If it does you have identified a priority training need – a need that lies within your 'key effectiveness area'. If there are no training implications for your selected issues, go back to (i) and examine the issues that have a lesser priority.

(iv) *Do your activities match your 'key effectiveness area'?*

The activities any trainer undertakes should naturally aim to help resolve key organizational issues. They should therefore lie mainly within the 'key effectiveness areas'. How appropriate are the activities you carry out?

List below the major activities that you have undertaken as part of your job over the last year and estimate what proportion of your time is spend on each.

ACTIVITIES	Estimated percentage of time spent on each activity	Rank order
1		
2		
3		
4		
5		
6		
7		
8		
9		
10		

Now rank the activities in terms of the time that you spent on them, highest first.

FACTORS INFLUENCING YOUR EFFECTIVENESS

Positive	Negative
e.g. good match between organizational needs and training actually carried out.	e.g. too much time spent on trivial area.
1	1
2	2
3	3

Taking positive action

How close is the match between (iv) and (ii)? Can you ensure a better match?

Are you in a position to decide what activities you should be carrying out or is this under someone else's control?

What other activities could you usefully be involved in?

C.   What approach do you adopt in your training activities?

Consistency in patterns of behaviour results in trainers having their own style of working. This is moulded by their own personal preferences as well as by the organization in which they work. For trainers to be effective, they must have an approach to training that fits in with the organizational culture. There are no right approaches *per se* – there are only more appropriate or less appropriate approaches for a given situation.

A number of dimensions can be used to characterize your trainer style:

1   Do you have an inclination to use trainer-centred approaches such as lecturing or learner-centred approaches such as discussion method? This may be conditioned by such factors as how skilful you are at handling a group of learners, conviction about the relative effectiveness of each approach and the willingness of learners to be actively involved.

2   Do you use your own powers of persuasion to get people interested and involved in training or do you use authority or the authority of others to get people involved? This may say something about the level of autocracy of the trainer or perhaps about the willingness of people in the organization to learn.

3   Do you work in a detached way or are you pervasive in the organization? This has important implications regarding how in touch you are with real organizational needs and problems. It perhaps also says something about your social skills.

4   Do you adopt a theory-centred approach to training or do you adopt a problem – or need-centred approach? The former approach is likely to be perceived as being academic, the latter possibly too narrow. A balanced approach is generally required.

5   Do you use interventionist strategies or do you always rely on a course-based solution. Learning opportunities may be presented in a variety of forms and it is sensible to explore the full range of options.

6   Are your primary concerns for the learners or for the organization? While any organization 'is its people' there is a

need to allocate effort where it will produce most benefit to the organization and therefore to the employees.

7   Do you respond automatically to training needs as presented to you or do you diagnose the nature of apparent training needs before responding? It is not always easy to question and analyse a need, particularly if it is a senior manager with a strong ownership of the problem or need. The skilful trainer will be able to get the person to analyse the need and perhaps better understand the problem.

8   Do you structure programmes highly or do you adopt a more flexible approach? Prestructuring to some extent will be an important part of effective planning of training. Overstructuring will mean that you will not adequately respond to learner's needs as they arise.

9   Do you use standard or tried approaches, or do you experiment with new or different training approaches? Variety may serve not only to motivate the learners but also yourself.

10   Do you tend to propose solutions or do you guide learners through problem solving? In many cases learners will be more convinced about solutions if they have had a hand in arriving at them.

11   Do you work strategically, planning ahead and setting objectives or do you work in an unsystematic way? Without a clear idea of training goals and method it is unlikely that you will make a significant contribution to the organization.

12   Do you take steps to remain up to date on subject matter and what is going on in the organization? You are unlikely to be effective if you do not.

13   Are you more concerned with conveying underlying principles or do you choose specific areas of need for training initiatives? This may reflect your underlying philosophy of training and its relationship to education.

14   Do you obtain feedback to improve your training or do you assume that you are doing a good job? Getting feedback should be an integral part of the job.

15   Do you vary the training approach to suit learners or do you in effect disregard their preferences? This again will reflect whether you have a learner-centred orientation or a trainer-centred orientation.

REVIEW	C. APPROACH TO TRAINING

Below are listed a number of dimensions that can be used to characterize the approach that trainers tend to adopt. Consider the way in which you do your job and put a cross in the appropriate place on each dimension. Then put a circle on each dimension to indicate the ideal position, bearing in mind the organization's needs.

DIMENSIONS OF TRAINERS STYLE:

1 Uses trainer-centred training approaches |_____| Uses learner-centred training approaches

2 Uses persuasion to get people involved in training |_____| Uses own authority or the authority of others to get people involved in training

3 Works in a detached way |_____| Is pervasive in the organization

4 Adopts theory-centred approaches in training |_____| Adopts problem-or-need centred approaches in training

5 Uses interventionist strategies |_____| Does not use interventionist strategies

6 Primary concern is for the needs of the organization |_____| Primary concern is for the needs of the individual

7 Responds to training needs as presented to him |_____| Diagnoses the nature of apparent training needs before responding

8 Structures training programmes highly |_____| Adopts a more flexible approach to training programme structure

9	Uses standard/tried solutions	├———————┤	Experiments with training approaches
10	Tends to propose solutions	├———————┤	Guides people through problem solving
11	Works strategically, plans ahead and sets objectives	├———————┤	Responds to problems and needs as they arise
12	Takes steps to remain informed on subject matter and the organization	├———————┤	Does not take steps to remain informed on subject matter and the organization
13	Chooses specific areas for training initiatives	├———————┤	Is more concerned with teaching principles
14	Obtains feedback to improve training	├———————┤	Is not concerned with obtaining feedback
15	Varies training approach to suit learners	├———————┤	Tends to use the same training approach, disregarding the type of learners

How much discrepancy is there between the style that is best suited to your organization's needs and the approach that you adopt? Can you reduce this gap?

FACTORS INFLUENCING YOUR EFFECTIVENESS

Positive	*Negative*
e.g. pervasive in the organization	e.g Narrow repertoire of training methods
1	1
2	2
3	3

Taking positive action

Does your general approach fit in with the organizational culture?

How can you make a better one?

Can you identify areas of specific weakness?

D. What knowledge and skills do you possess?

What knowledge and skills does a trainer need to be able to do the job effectively? Inevitably trainers need a broad range of knowledge and skills, with particular types being important in particular situations. However, there is a general acceptance that trainers need a range of 'core competencies'. The Manpower Services Commission (1978) defines core competencies as:

> ... the individual skills and knowledge required by training specialists so that they can
>
> (i)   carry out their initial role effectively in their organizations, and
>
> (ii) have a basis for developing their roles and their performance.

It proposes two sets of core competencies – common areas of know-how and areas of specific knowledge and skills.

COMMON AREAS OF KNOW-HOW	AREAS OF SPECIFIC KNOWLEDGE
1 The organization and its business.	1 Direct training element.
2 The training function and training specialist roles.	2 Planning and organizing element.
3 Learning and design of training	3 Determining or managing element.
4 Diagnosis and problem solving.	4 Consulting and advisory element.
5 People in organizations.	

In our research we asked trainers and managers to identify the skills that they would expect trainers to have. The findings were as follows:

TRAINER VIEWPOINT	%
Communication and presentation skills	33
Analytical skills, intelligence, logic, clarity of thought, ability to stand back and work strategically	29
Knowledge of subject matter	27
Adaptability, flexibility	20
Leadership skills, group control skills, social skills	18

MANAGER VIEWPOINT	%
Ability to hold learners' interest, ability to motivate people	49
Communication and presentation skills	45
Knowledge of subject matter, ability to relate training to practice	39
Ability to use good examples	28
Group control skills, social skills	24

The findings demonstrate a good measure of agreement between trainers and managers on the general competencies a trainer would be expected to have.

The sets of knowledge and skills that trainers need will be determined by the role that they take on in the organization. One has only to think about the different knowledge and skills needed by, for instance, a direct trainer, a training manager, a writer and designer of open learning materials and a training consultant.

Skill and knowledge demands are likely to be influenced by such factors as:

- how specialized is the area of training;
- the level of staff you have to deal with;
- whether you are acting in the capacity of an 'expert' or 'facilitator', and
- whether you are responsible for being a self-starter or you are directed by someone else.

What we should be doing is identifying the knowledge and skill profile for a particular role and assessing trainers to see how closely they match a given profile.

REVIEW	D. KNOWLEDGE AND SKILLS

Think about the needs of your organization and the role that you are called upon to perform. List the main areas of knowledge and skills that are required to perform the role effectively.

Knowledge areas	*Skill areas*
_____	_____
_____	_____
_____	_____
_____	_____
_____	_____
_____	_____

How do you match up to the requirements?

FACTORS INFLUENCING YOUR EFFECTIVENESS

Positive	Negative
e.g. good group dynamics skills	e.g. finds difficulty in dealing with senior staff
1	1
2	2
3	3

Taking positive action

Having identified areas of lack of knowledge or skills, what can you do? Lack of knowledge can probably be helped by reading appropriate publications or going through open learning materials. Skill development will probably require help from a trainer training specialist in order to give you practice in the skill required.

E.   What characteristics do you possess?

What characteristics would one expect an effective trainer to have? No doubt most of us can think back to a trainer of some description whom we liked and who stimulated our interest in the subject matter. What is it about the person that created this effect?

We found a high degree of consistency in what the research had to say. Two personal characteristics stand out for effective trainers:

1   they are *SENSITIVE* and *RESPONSIVE* to the learners' needs, and
2   they are genuinely *INTERESTED* in the subject area.

Underlying the first set of characteristics is a keen eye to learning difficulties and a desire to want to help. More mature learners are particularly reluctant to make obvious any learning difficulties that they have. It takes a perceptive trainer to recognize the situation and a sensitive one to respond without harming the esteem of the learner.

Whether a trainer is interested in the subject matter will be obvious to learners from the beginning and may influence their level of motivation to learn. It is difficult to see how a trainer not interested in the subject matter can do a truly effective job.

A variety of other characteristics were mentioned as being desirable – patience, humour, confidence, toleration of ambiguity, credibility and others.

In some ways, credibility is an unusual factor to mention because it is not really a direct characteristic of trainers, but something that may be attributed to them by others. It is related to reputation.

But what makes a trainer credible? There seem to be two stages at which credibility is attributed or denied to a trainer. For new trainers, initial credibility seems to be based on the reputation they bring with them from a previous job. This may be related to past experience, achievements, age, contacts etc. Later trainer credibility is based on direct knowledge of the quality and usefulness of the services the trainer can provide. It also relates to the level of trust in them.

Baird (1980) defines credibility as the willingness of one individual to believe another individual. He suggests that it is not a unified judgement people make, but is arrived at by reference to a number of dimensions. In relation to managerial credibility, he describes six dimensions – competency, character, intent, dynamism, personality and 'admirability'. The findings on trainer credibility support this notion. Judgements are based on a number of dimensions very similar to those for judging managerial effectiveness.

It is probable that trainer credibility assumes such importance as an issue because the trainer's role is frequently vague. Because trainers by the nature of their work have a message or information to convey, they are frequently in the position of having to persuade others about its value or the value of the activities in which they are engaging. The level of credibility they are attributed is a reflection of the extent to which they succeed.

REVIEW	E. CHARACTERISTICS AND CREDIBILITY

How sensitive are you to learners' needs?

How responsive are you to learners' needs?

Are you genuinely interested in the subject matter of your training, or do you do the training because you have to?

Are you perceived as being a credible trainer? Indications of this would include frequent requests for help with training.

FACTORS INFLUENCING YOUR EFFECTIVENESS

Positive	*Negative*
e.g. frequently seeks feedback on training	e.g. credibility low due to poor performance in a training programme
1	1
2	2
3	3

Taking positive action

Personal characteristics are probably the most difficult things to change. However, an important starting point is to 'know yourself and how others see you'.

F.   What are the outcomes of your training activities?

The outcomes of trainer activity may be an important factor in determining your future effectiveness. They influence the level of credibility that is attributed and may determine the level of support and cooperation that is forthcoming from other staff. Once a track-record has been established it is difficult and sometimes impossible to change.

Outcomes of trainer activity may be judged at a variety of levels:

1   at 'enjoyment' level, following a training event;
2   looking at whether the learning objectives for the training event have been achieved;
3   looking at whether the job performance of the learners has been improved in the real job situation, and
4   looking at the contribution of training to the organization achieving its objectives.

As we move from level one to level four so it becomes progressively more difficult to relate outcomes to trainer influence. Many other factors confuse the picture. Inevitably this is why most trainers, irrespective of what type of trainers they are, will be judged on the outcomes of their direct training activities.

REVIEW	F. OUTCOMES

Look back over the last year or two. No doubt some of the outcomes of your training activities were more successful than others. List them in the appropriate column.

More successful activities		*Less successful activities*	
1	_____	1	_____
2	_____	2	_____
3	_____	3	_____
4	_____	4	_____
5	_____	5	_____

On what basis do you judge success?

Are there more activities that had successful outcomes than unsuccessful outcomes?

Has this affected your reputation as a trainer?

FACTORS INFLUENCING YOUR EFFECTIVENESS

Positive	*Negative*
e.g. particularly good outcomes for the organization of a specific training event.	e.g. carrying on with a training programme that produces no apparent benefits
1	1
2	2
3	3

Taking positive action

Publish positive training outcomes so that people recognize the contribution that training is making.

Regularly review the outcomes of training activities so that these may be improved.

G.   How does the organization influence the trainer?

Trainer effectiveness is largely determined by the abilities that trainers have, their work behaviour and determination. It is also influenced greatly by the context in which they work – the organization can enhance or reduce their effectiveness.

What then are the main organizational factors that prevent or help trainers to be effective?

- *The level of support for training.*
  It is difficult in many cases to make generalizations about the level of support for training. People have a range of attitudes and in some ways an organization may support training but in another way it may reject it. However, the level of support for training will be reflected in such factors as the resources given to the training function, the authority given to trainers, their position in the hierarchy and the day-to-day co-operation trainers get from managers. In some cases there may be intellectual and verbal support for the notion of training, but little practical commitment.

- *The demand for training.*
  The demand for training may exist because of mandatory reasons, such as the training of pilots in an airline or of safety officers in an engineering company. It may exist because of the nature of the business or the absence of suitably qualified people in the market place. Perhaps job performance is poor. The trainer will not be in a position to identify all training needs and managers should be directly involved in this.

- *Managerial style and sophistication.*
  Managers may or may not appreciate the benefits that can be derived from training. They may be too preoccupied with other activities to give consideration to training.

- *Expectations.*
  A history of training activity in the organization may build up an expectation for training. Expectations may limit the range of activities trainers can engage in and the role they would like to develop.

- *Reputation of the training function.*
  A positive demonstration of benefits of training in the organization will serve to convince people about its potential value. A poor reputation will hinder the work of the trainer

and make it almost impossible to get co- operation.
- *Other factors.*
These may include the relationship between the training function and the personnel function, the prosperity of the organization, how rapidly the organization is changing and the level of recruitment as well as other factors.

REVIEW	G. ORGANIZATIONAL FACTORS

Do the following organizational factors influence your effectiveness?

- the level of support for training
- the demand for training
- managerial style and sophistication
- expectations
- reputation of the training function

Are any other factors influential?

FACTORS INFLUENCING YOUR EFFECTIVENESS

Positive	*Negative*
e.g. managers willing to get involved in training activities	e.g. low level of resources given to training function
1	1
2	2
3	3

Taking positive action

What steps can you take to gain the organization's increased commitment to training?

Do you nurture relationships with key people in the organization?

Do you 'sell' the benefits of training? Do you try to integrate training into the day-to-day activities of the business?

SUMMARY

Trainer effectiveness cannot be defined in a simple way. It is conditioned by a number of key factors. These are:

- how trainers see their role and responsibilities;
- on what activities trainers spend their time;
- what approach trainers adopt in their activities;
- what knowledge and skills trainers possess;
- what are the outcomes of trainers' activities, and
- how the organization influences trainers.

The relative importance of these factors will be conditioned by the organizational context. Look back at the positive and negative factors you have listed that affect your effectiveness. Is there any pattern? Are the negative factors ones that you can do anything about? How can you build on the positive factors?

The following chapters take some of the issues raised here and look at them in more depth.

REFERENCES/FURTHER READING

Source material

Some of the material in this chapter is based upon the results of a study carried out for the UK's Manpower Services Commission and already referred to in Chapter 1. In addition to the source quoted in Chapter 1, the following may be of interest:

Bennett, R., 'The Effective Trainer', *Training and Development*, August, 1983.

Bennett, R., 'How to Survive As A Trainer', *Journal of European Industrial Training*, 1985, vol. 9, no. 6.

Bennett, R. and Leduchowicz, T., *A Report on the Trainer Effectiveness Project*. Thames Valley Regional Management Centre, 1982.

Leduchowicz, T., *Guide to Trainer Effectiveness*. Manpower Services Commission/Institute of Training and Development, 1984.

Additional references

Baird, J.E., 'Enhancing Managerial Credibility', *Personnel Journal*, 1980.

Manpower Services Commission, *First Report of the Training of Trainers Committee*, UK, 1978.

Nadler, L., 'The Variety of Training Roles', *Industrial and Commercial Training*, 1969, vol. 1, no. 1.

3 The Right Role

Roger Bennett

Given the changing circumstances of many organizations and the number of factors that influence trainer effectiveness that we have considered in the previous chapters, developing the right role is crucial: it may not be easy. Identifying the most appropriate role may in itself be difficult: changing to that role from another might be seen by some trainers as almost impossible. If you, as a trainer, have been working successfully for many years in a way that suits you, why change anyway? Why shouldn't you continue doing what you are good at, and let someone else take on the new initiatives, cope with the changing demands, and fight the power battles in the organization?

That of course, is an option, but it may not be one that either you or your organization can afford. You may have to adapt or change, or leave. But this is an extreme position that not all trainers will find themselves in. However, because demands and needs are changing, you must at least think through the role you are in and whether you should and can adopt a different role. The purpose of this chapter is to provide you with some frameworks and guidance that will help you do this 'thinking through'. This is very necessary, because experience and research shows that successful trainers do, from time-to-time, have to think about what they do and have to assess critically whether what they do is still relevant. The 'what am I here for' question is the key to unlocking the door to your future success.

ONE ROLE OR MANY?

Given that the nature of the work of most trainers is very much concerned with direct training, is it sensible to even consider that there is any role other than that of instructor? Clearly, it is sensible, as your own experience will no doubt confirm. The very obvious difference between the work of a training officer and that of a training manager is one with which we are all familiar. There will be some overlap: many training managers do some teaching or instructing, and training officers often have resources and people to manage. But the differences are there to be seen. Even people carrying out similar activities do them in different ways because of differences in background, experience, personality, preferences and organization pressures. So, one training officer may do more work with individuals, while another may be happiest when lecturing to large groups.

We can therefore state, as a general principle, that there is no one role of a trainer but a variety of roles within the trainer's job. The number of roles contained within any one job will be limited, not least by the demands of the job itself or the expectations of others. Thus, the training manager may be expected to act as a consultant to line managers and the training officer may be required to act as an innovator in developing approaches to solving organizational problems and as an administrator of training programmes. But what are the various roles the trainer might adopt?

DIFFERENT APPROACHES TO THE TRAINING ROLE

Quite a number of different ways have been suggested for looking at what trainers do. These usually have been in the form of 'role classifications'. Many of them are similar, or contain types of role/ jobs that are the same. They are based on studies of the work trainers do in countries as far apart as Singapore, the UK and the USA. We shall not review and discuss each one here – they can be followed-up through the suggested reading at the end of this chapter.

What emerges from these different approaches is that

1   there are quite different things that different trainers do, or that the same trainer does on different occasions, and
2   there is no one best role.

To produce a framework that helps us think more clearly about these issues, we have drawn together the common themes that emerge from the various approaches to looking at trainer roles. This we now describe.

A GENERAL STATEMENT OF ROLES

There are five key roles that emerge from the various classifications of what trainers do. Two are mainly concerned with maintaining levels of performance, two are concerned with initiating and coping with change, while the fifth is more managerial and links with the other four. They can be described as follows:

1   *The trainer* – a training role that is primarily concerned with actual direct training. It is a role that involves the trainer in helping people to learn, providing feedback about their learning and adopting course designs to meet trainees' needs. The 'trainers' role may involve classroom teaching and instruction, laboratory work, small group work, supervision of individual project work and all those activities that directly influence immediate learning experiences. In effect, the trainer is a learning specialist.
2   *The provider* – a training role that is primarily concerned with the design, maintenance and delivery of training programmes. It will involve training needs analysis, setting objectives, designing courses, choosing appropriate methods, testing out courses, evaluating courses or training activities and helping trainers to deliver the training.
3   *The consultant* – a training role that is primarily concerned with analysing business problems and assessing/recommending solutions, some of which may require training. It may involve some elements of the 'provider' role but specifically concentrates on liaising with line managers, identifying their performance problems, advising on possible training solutions (where appropriate), working with providers

and/or trainers to establish training programmes, advising training managers (where the roles are separated) on training goals and policies and ensuring evaluation takes place and the results are used.

4   *The innovator* – a training role that is primarily concerned with helping organizations effectively to manage change and solve performance problems. It will involve working with managers at senior/middle levels, providing support and help to managers in coping with change, identifying where seminars and workshops can be a useful means of educating managers for change and 'facilitating' change coming about, identifying the real sources of power in the organization and linking with these to help bring about change, and advising the training function on how it can best help in the change process. (In Organization Development terms, such a role might be called 'change agent', 'catalyst', or 'interventionist'). The role frequently overlaps with that of 'consultant'.

5   *The manager* – a training role that is primarily concerned with planning, organizing, controlling and developing the training and development activity or function. It will involve setting training goals, policies and plans; liaising with other departments and with senior managers about the contribution training can and should make to improving performance; ensuring that appropriate training activities are designed, developed, delivered and evaluated; acquiring and developing training staff; establishing effective lines of authority and communication within the training function; acquiring and effectively using non-staff resources; monitoring quality standards, and controlling activities against a total training plan. Some 'provider' roles may contain elements of the 'manager' role in small organizations or in situations where providers have several training programmes to deliver.

These roles are not distinct 'packages' of activities, behaviours and responsibilities. They each have a clear focus but do relate to each other, as already indicated in the descriptions given above. The manager role has a strong link with all others, by virtue of its very nature. Trainer and Provider roles are more concerned with maintenance activities whilst those of Consultant and Innovator are (often) involved with change and problem solving. These links can be depicted as shown in Figure 3.1.

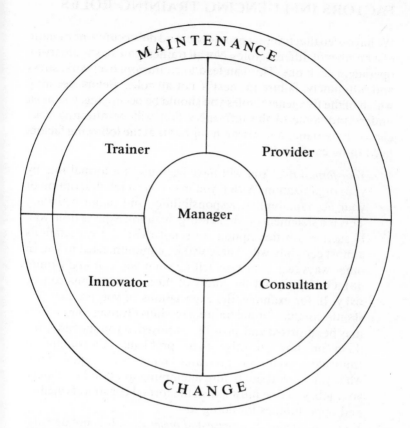

Figure 3:1 General Trainer Roles

The question now remains as to which role or roles you should be occupying. Before considering this, we need to look at the factors that influence your role.

REMEMBER – NO PARTICULAR ROLE IS BETTER THAN ANY OTHER, IN GENERAL. IT ALL DEPENDS ON YOUR SITUATION.

FACTORS INFLUENCING TRAINING ROLES

We have seen that training people can, and do, occupy one or more of a number of different roles. Not all trainers can, or should try to, operate in each one. This can lead to confusion, overwork, stress and, ultimately, failure in most if not all roles. Before deciding which of the five general roles you should be occupying, you must understand some of the influences that will be affecting your choice. Experience and research suggest that the following factors need to be considered:

1. *Your formal role.* You will have been given a formal role by your organization. With it you may have a job description of your accountabilities, responsibilities and major activities. This is a statement of what the organization expects from you. If such a job description does not exist, the expectations almost certainly will. These will be communicated to you in other ways (e.g. your boss telling what you can and cannot do). Going beyond the limits of these expectations can be risky. If, for example, the expectations of you are that you should conduct formal training sessions (Trainer role), others may be surprised and, possibly, annoyed, if you start advising them on how to solve their problems (Consultant or Innovator), even if the pressures facing them suggest that is what you should do. Before attempting to extend or change your job, you first must assess the formal constraints against and opportunities for doing so.

2. *Your own training experience and preferences.* It is not unusual for people in training and development to have a preferred role and way of doing things. You may, for example, have been operating as a Provider for many years in a fairly stable environment, and with considerable success. You have been appointed or selected to do it because of your training and experience, and you probably find it very satisfying. Adopting a different role may require you to acquire new or additional skills and to operate in a way that is not familiar or comfortable to you. You will make the change successfully *only* if you have the capacity and support to acquire these skills and operate in unfamiliar settings or with new approaches and methods. The change might initially be a little uncomfortable but, given the need to change, a

willingness to change and the necessary support, it is
possible.

3   *Expectations and attitudes of managers and clients.* As well as the
     expectations built into the job and your own view of it, others
     in the organization will have expectations about and
     attitudes towards people in training and what they should/
     should not do. Where managers make genuinely positive and
     encouraging noises about training, where they see a possible
     direct contribution to organizational needs and where a
     change in *your* role would be in line with *their* problems and
     requirements, you are likely to get at least tacit support and at
     best real commitment. Some companies demonstrate such
     positive attitudes, while many others do not. Find out how
     things are in your organization before trying to adapt or
     change what you do. A simple test is to invite managers to
     take part in a training event as a contributor, at least on two
     occasions. If they decline, you probably have little real
     support out there.

4   *The culture of your organization.* This is concerned with the
     typical approaches to doing things and the values, attitudes
     and relationships among people. There are several different
     ways of describing culture, but two extremes will illustrate it.
     Some organizations operate in very bureaucratic ways – rules,
     procedures, written standards and regulations, etc., for almost
     everything. A formal approach to work is adopted. It is likely
     that in such a culture a highly innovative, flexible, change-
     driven training operation will be given a tough ride, as will the
     training people. The reverse is also to be found – adaptive,
     flexible cultures where people matter more than paperwork.
     In this type of environment a highly structured approach to
     training might not be acceptable.

5   *The needs of your organization.* Training people do not exist
     because of some form of divine organizational right. They are
     there – you are there – because the organization has goals to
     achieve, needs to be satisfied and problems to be solved as we
     have seen in Chapter 2. You must be making your own unique
     contribution to these requirements. If you are not, you
     shouldn't be there at all. How best to make that contribution
     is a matter of judgement, based on assessment of the needs. If,
     for example, the organization has taken on a lot of new

clerical staff with little experience of wordprocessing, and is
going into word processing in a big way, you have a major
requirement for training people who will act as Providers and
Trainers. If, however, your company has just merged with
another, and the two have very different styles of management
and operating procedures, you could be faced with some
massive consulting and innovating requirements. Your role
must, therefore, respond to the needs of the business, the
organizations, the institution . . . . . that employs you to give it
help and support. For Training Managers this is of critical
importance. If you cannot adopt the required role, at least
make sure you have some key people around you who
can.

6   *The chances of success.* Adopting a new role that has little
chance of some reasonably early success will be futile. It may
be positively dangerous to 'go for broke' with a radically new
approach and nothing to fall back on. One Training Manager
who did this, and lost most of his trainers, said afterwards that
he had learned not to put all his eggs in one basket. He had
become, almost exclusively, an Innovator. When a change
occurred at senior management level that led to a demand for
more of the Trainer and Provider roles, he became isolated.
Your chances of success must influence you in adopting the
right role. Your chances of success will also be influenced by
the power structure in the organization. You need to be
politically aware, if not active. You may well need the support
of others in operating your new role.

7   *Changing circumstances.* As we have seen in Chapter 1, the
changing circumstances of many companies is forcing a re-
think about training itself and about the roles training people
should play in contributing to organizational success. You
will need to change and adopt your role. This may be in small
ways or in more radical terms. A regular review of your role
and your contribution to organizational excellence will do
you a power of good. Changing from, say, a Provider to an
Innovator to meet a serious challenge from the competition
in the market place will not necessarily be permanent. After
the challenge has been seen off, you may have to revert to the
Provider role. Change is seldom a once-off occurrence, so you
should review your role quite regularly.

Thus, a number of key factors will influence your role. You need to consider them all, and others that may be unique to your particular situation. What you need to do is to carry out a thorough review of your role.

REVIEWING YOUR ROLE

You cannot adopt a new role or modify your existing role in the dark. You will need some basic information – answers to key questions that will help you decide whether or not your current role is still appropriate. The key questions are these:

1   have the real business needs of the organization changed recently?
2   if yes to 1), have the policies and plans necessary for meeting these needs changed?
3   if yes to 2) have the purposes of the training function changed?
4   if yes to 3), is your current role still valid or appropriate?

If the answer to 4) is yes, you may be operating a flexible role, or you may be deluding yourself. If it is 'no', you will need to do something about your role. To help you assess the extent of what you may need to do, work through the Role Review Cycle shown in Figure 3.2. The top left hand loop (A) assumes your answers to questions 1), 2) and 3) are all 'no'. Loop B helps you decide if your current role requires extending. That is, it may need some other elements added to it. Loop C is based on the need to make a major shift. This can be by adding a further role (e.g. you are a Trainer who needs also to become a Provider), or adopting a completely new role (e.g. you are a Provider who needs to become a Consultant instead). As you will see, loops B and C consider the need for new skills. Such skills may well be crucial to your success in the role.

The rest of this chapter will look at ways in which you can more fully assess the nature of your current role and the role you might need to adopt. It will also look at how you might be able to improve your influence within the organization.

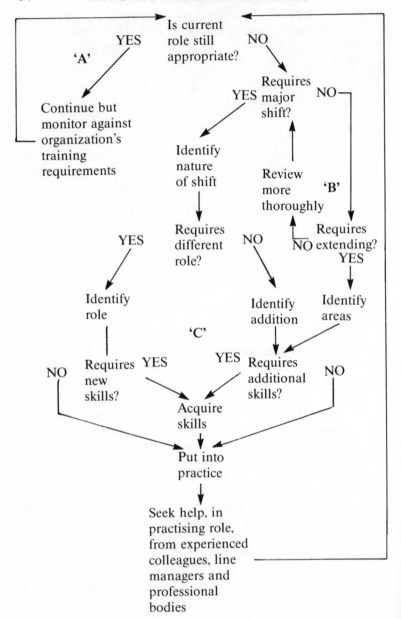

Figure 3:2 Role review cycle

WHICH ROLE(S) DO YOU/SHOULD YOU PERFORM?

Listed below are a number of items that describe different facets of the roles training personnel operate. They are based on the general statement of roles presented earlier in this chapter. There are also two columns, headed 'Do now' and 'Should do'. For each item, give a rating out of 10 under each of these column headings. A rating of 10 would indicate that you do (or should do) a lot of that item; a rating of 0 (i.e. zero) that you do (or should do) none of that item. Ratings between these extremes can be used to indicate varying amounts. For example, against 'classroom teaching or instructing' you might have put '3' under the 'Do now' column, and '8' under the 'Should do' column. This would indicate that you feel your role should contain more of this item in the near future. Remember, you are trying to assess how and to what extent your role might need to be extended, added to or changed. Write your score on the lines provided. Ignore the lines against the 'Total score' items. We shall return to these later on.

Table 3:1
Role analysis questionnaire

	Item	Do now	Should do
A	classroom teaching or instructing	____	____
	small group work/seminars	____	____
	role playing or other simulations	____	____
	supervising individual project work	____	____
	adapting course/training designs	____	____
	researching your training/teaching subject	____	____
	choosing and using specific learning methods	____	____
	Total score	____	____

	Item	Do now	Should do
B	designing training courses/programmes	———	———
	identifying training needs	———	———
	setting course/programmes objectives	———	———
	choosing appropriate delivery methods	———	———
	identifying contributors to the training	———	———
	pilot-testing courses/programmes	———	———
	evaluating courses/programmes	———	———
	Total score	———	———
C	helping analyse business/performance problems	———	———
	recommending/assessing solutions	———	———
	identifying where training can help	———	———
	liaising with managers	———	———
	advising managers on training issues	———	———
	helping set up appropriate training	———	———
	working to implement training solutions	———	———
	Total score	———	———
D	identifying changing business priorities	———	———
	helping managers cope with change	———	———
	advising trainers on how to meet change	———	———
	working with managers to solve problems	———	———
	helping managers with training their staff	———	———
	bringing in external experts to help	———	———
	suggesting new ways of developing staff	———	———
	Total score	———	———
E	setting training goals and priorities	———	———
	establishing a training plan	———	———
	acquiring training resources	———	———
	developing training resources	———	———
	liaising with other departments	———	———
	monitoring training standards	———	———
	controlling budgets and activities	———	———
	Total score	———	———

Now add up the ratings under each column heading within each grouping of items (i.e. A, B, etc) and put the result on the lines opposite 'Total score'. When you have a complete set of five 'Total scores' under each column, do the following:

1   for the 'Do now' column, rank order your set of 'Total score', where rank order 1 would be the highest score;
2   for the 'Should do' column, repeat 1) above;
3   write down on a piece of paper the group letters, with the appropriate rank number for each column against them. For example, it might look as follows:

Grouping	Ranking	
	Do now	*Should do*
A	1	3
B	5	2
C	4	1
D	3	4
E	2	5

In this fictitious (in fact, purely random) example, group A seems to be the dominant current role (followed by E), whereas group C would seem to be the role our fictitious training specialist should be adopting in the near future. Joint ranking i.e. equal 'Total score' values, would have indicated combined or joint roles. The roles indicated by each grouping are as follows:

A – Trainer
B – Provider
C – Consultant
D – Innovator
E – Manager.

Remember, these are not mutually exclusive categories. They do, however, give the main emphasis of each role. Which were your dominant roles in each column? Is there a major change involved? (i.e. two quite different roles indicated). Are several roles closely related i.e. are the scores fairly close? Answering these questions will help determine what you may need to do.

4   Return to the Role Review Cycle (Figure 3.2). Work through it
again. Does it suggest a similar kind of change, in terms of
extent, as the above? Here we are looking at the nature or
content of the change as well as the extent of it – in Figure 3.2
only the extent of change is highlighted.

5   If you can, review your analysis with your boss, a colleague, or
a friend. Does it really reflect what you now do and what you
should do? Remember, it is only a guide. It is not a
scientifically valid instrument.

GETTING THE RIGHT EXPERIENCE

By now you will have established where you are and where you
should be going. The process of getting from one to the other may
require simple actions (such as trying out an additional set of
items or activities) or fairly systematic development (such as a self-
development programme or going on a workshop). Exactly what
you do should be the subject of discussion between yourself and
your boss or some other (friendly) helper. Here are some of the
things you might consider doing:

1   *Experiment* – there are sometimes opportunities to try out
elements of a new or extended role. For example, if you are a
Trainer, you may well receive requests for help in laying on
specific courses for the subordinates of a manager who had
been on one of the courses you had taught on. Favourably
impressed with your performance, he rings you to see if you
can do something to, say, develop broader thinking in the way
his/her staff do their work. This is a chance for you to
experiment with the Provider role. Or, as a Manager, a
departmental head asks you to visit him to discuss some
problems he has. He feels training might be part of the
solution. Here is an opportunity for you to try out the
Consultant role. You may be able to initiate opportunities for
yourself. Thus, visiting a number of managers to review the
training provision will in itself give experience of the
Consultant role. It may lead to possibilities for innovation.
However and wherever the opportunities arise, take them if
you feel they offer real possibilities and do not contain too
many risks or threats.

2   *Work with others* – although the 'apprenticeship' approach to training seems to be a little out of favour these days, it has much to offer training personnel who wish to experience new roles with the help and support of someone experienced in the role in question. Working with external consultants (in your organization or elsewhere) can be beneficial. So, too, can working with an experienced and well-regarded professional from your own organization. Trainers who need to acquire experience of, say, the Provider role, will gain much from working with a really good, professional course organizer on a particular project. Having worked through the issues and problems side-by-side, running solo is not so daunting. This applies equally to the methods and techniques of training as well as to roles. A Trainer who has done little else but direct training may feel reluctant to try out role play or pure workshop technique. Co-tutoring with an experienced practitioner will give valuable experience on which to decide whether or not to try such techniques without that kind of back-up, support and advice.

3   *Job swaps* – these entail moving from your current job to another within the training function to gain experience of a new role. It can be for a short period (say three months) or a longer period (up to a year). You will need to do this on a planned and negotiated basis. Make sure you have a proper set of work activities with real responsibility. Being someone's 'help mate' will not do. You need experience and should not be a spare pair of hands. Get a proper job plan. Get involved in the real 'meat' of the job. Keep a diary of what you do and the lessons/experiences gained. Note any areas in which you might need training or development yourself. Use the 'work with others' approach to add to your experience and to gain confidence. On return to your previous job, negotiate areas of work in which you can use the new role to good effect. Resist pressures to revert to doing exactly the same work as before. That will prove very frustrating!

4   *Exchange jobs* – this can be done internally with another training department (if the company is big enough), with a sister company, or with an external organization. The same rules for 3) above apply here. There may be a temptation to stay if the job goes well. If your parent company is sincere in

allowing you to operate your new role when you return, then do return. If it isn't, you may be well advised to accept a new job. This should, however, be resisted. The exchange will involve someone from your new outfit taking your job for the period of the exchange, and that person may wish to return. You might arrange a number of meetings with that person, during the exchange, to compare notes and learn from each other. A variant of this might be a secondment to an external company.

5   *Action learning* – this is an effective way of gaining new experience. It involves carrying out an action-based project on how to develop and implement your new role. Visits, interviews and action planning are all important elements. If several trainers are also changing roles, form yourselves into a group (or 'set' as it is called) to help one another. Get an experienced Trainer or Consultant to act as a set adviser for what you do. Write up your experiences, findings and conclusions, develop an action plan for your new role, and present it to the set (invite your boss along too). Your project should be agreed to and sponsored by your boss.

6   *Seminars and workshops* – these can be useful for getting away from work-based restraints and thinking through your new role. Don't attend any that are too academic. Those based on analysing your job and preparing a development or action plan are to be preferred. Examples of seminars/workshops for reviewing trainer role and effectiveness are given in Appendix A. They are based on actual designs that have proved to be very successful. Organizations such as ASTD, BACIE and ITD can give you information about relevant workshops.

7   *Open learning programmes* – more and more open learning programmes for trainers are becoming available. They allow you to analyse your job, acquire new learning and make action plans at your own pace. Tutorial support is often made available. You will need an internal adviser or 'mentor' to help you work through key organizational issues. A good example of such a programme is that developed by the Trainer Support Services of the ITD. It comprises a video, a set of workbooks and a supplementary pack of information. It is very much an individual approach, based on self-

development. Although designed for Training Managers, other trainers may also benefit from it.

GAINING INFLUENCE THROUGH YOUR ROLE

Developing an effective role may well involve more than deciding what you should be doing and how you can gain experience in your new role. In changing or moving from one role to another, or in extending your role in a big way, you will almost certainly experience a need to influence other people. Moving round the trainer role wheel in Figure 3.1 almost certainly involves different requirements to influence other people. Thus, the Trainer must influence trainees to undertake particular activities or exercises; the Provider must influence trainers and others to instruct, teach or co-tutor on programmes; the Consultant must influence managers to seek advice or to listen to recommendations; the Innovator must influence managers to get involved with problems and allow training to help; and the Manager must influence staff and clients to work together to make training more effective – these, and many others, are examples of influence in and through the five general roles.

But what is 'influence'? It is a well-known and often used word. We use phrases such as: 'the secretary has considerable influence with her boss' or 'the general manager must have influence with the Board if he gets his own way so often'. What we are talking about here is a subtle, almost unnoticed, form of persuasion to get people to do things for us (or for themselves or somebody else). Trainers very often need to do this, because of their position and status in the organization.

But how? In what ways can trainers bring influence to bear in the roles they – you – perform? We know from experience and research that influence can stem from a number of different sources. What we shall do is to describe some of these sources, and then see if and how you can call upon them to make your job more effective.

Sources of influence

Formal position

Many jobs are based on a formal, written set of duties, responsibilities, relationships and authority. This is particularly so in large, bureaucratic organizations. It constitutes the formal position of the job holder and confers on that person a degree of influence. Within the limits of the job description, the person can make decisions and initiate actions. Within the training function, some trainers wil be able to gain a certain degree of influence over, say, course design. Outside the function, however, the influence will be limited. This is often because training is considered to be a peripheral activity, not a line activity. Where training is effectively represented at Board level, the influence may be greater. Mostly, trainers will have to look to other sources of influence to make things happen.

Tradition

Most organizations have well established ways of doing things that have developed over a number of years. Such a tradition can exert powerful limits on what people can do. If the tradition is against a training role other than Trainer, Provider or Manager, gaining influence through a new role can be difficult. Working to change tradition can be effective if you can gain access to and influence over key people.

Rewards and sanctions

The ability to give rewards and impose sanctions can be a real source of influence. Line managers and union officers typically have that ability. Trainers and other staff personnel typically do not, unless they control certain budgets. Where they do, they may be able to offer inducements of a fairly limited form.

Higher authority

It is often possible to secure influence over others by appealing to higher authority e.g. the managing director. This requires a sound working relationship of a formal or informal nature. Again, a training director at Board level might be able to achieve this. Otherwise, it depends on cultivating a strong informal relationship with someone perceived to have power in the organization. While this can bring about influence, a danger lies in the possibility of changes in the power relationship e.g. the power figure leaving or being removed, leaving you isolated. Better to work through several power figures.

Political access

In some respects this is similar to the above. It may, however, involve securing links with and access to powerful groups, particularly those who have control over resources or pay awards or promotions. It requires an awareness of the state of politics in the organization. You need to know what the score is and to have an understanding of how political power can change.

Expertise

This is probably a major source of influence for trainers. The respect accorded a high level of expertise can produce a situation where others will listen to you, take note of what you say and be prepared to act on it. When taking on a new role, you will need to develop quickly the expertise associated with that role before you can use it to good effect. The extent of the influence gained will depend on how acceptable or legitimate it is in the eyes of those you wish to influence. If they don't see it as legitimate or useful expertise, they may ignore your advice and recommendations. This is particularly so for Consultants and Innovators.

Credibility

This is concerned with the extent to which people are prepared to believe and accept what you have to offer. It links with expertise and is built upon your past successes. Credibility has to be earned, by what you have done in the past (your track record) and what you are now able to do. It is about 'being able to deliver the goods'. So, in building credibility, start with those activities that can bring visible successes that will earn you initial respect – and then repeat them.

Personality

Many trainers find that a friendly, dynamic, open personality is an advantage. The ability to persuade others through the force of personality is well known to sales people and industrial relations experts, among others. But there must be a fit between the personalities involved otherwise personal clashes may ensue. Managers, Consultants and Innovators often find personality to be a major influencing factor. If your personality does not 'fit' you will have to work on other sources of influence e.g. expertise.

Access to information and resources

Where it is possible to develop such access, your influence can be considerable. Developing friendly working relationships with those who control information and resources is a vital part of the process. This brings in, to some extent, other means of gaining influence, such as political access. The one may depend on the other. Managers of the training function will often have to develop this kind of influence in order to secure resources for and acceptance of new trainer roles. They will also need access to information to be able to keep abreast of what is happening in the organization and so decide in what areas they can apply new trainer roles.

Coalition

This refers to the mobilization of other people in the organization to support the things you want to do. The ability to mobilize support will depend in part on your political access. You will need friends and allies, sometimes in high places, to get a coalition moving. If such key influencers of opinion are persuaded of the relevance and importance of your case, you will be in a strong position. There are dangers, though. Coalitions can result in 'opposing camps', and if the camp you are in loses out, you could be in the wilderness. How closely linked you become to a particular camp must rest on your own reading of the situation. Using coalitions is however, less risky than being too dependent on one individual – however powerful that person might be. Fortunes change, and if yours are linked too firmly with one person, his demise could also be yours.

Identifying the right source of influence

These, then, are some of the most important sources of influence available to trainers to improve the effectiveness of their role. Clearly, not all sources will be available to all trainers operating all roles. Experience suggests that the sources available for each role are likely to be as shown in Table 3.2.

Table 3:2
Influence sources and relevant roles

Source of Influence	TRAINING ROLE				
	Trainer	Provider	Consultant	Innovator	Manager
Access to information			X	X	X
Access to resources			X	X	X
Coalition		?	X	X	X
Credibility	X	X	X	X	X
Expertise	X	X	X	X	X
Formal position		?	?	?	X
Higher authority	X	X	X	X	X
Personality	X	X	X	X	X
Political access		?	X	X	X
Rewards			?	?	?
Sanctions					?
Tradition					?

The sources of influence have been listed in the table in alphabetical order to reduce the possibility of one source being seen as more important than another. Importance depends very much on availability of the source and what it can do for you. Each source is given a symbol (X or ?) to denote its likely availability to each role. A (X) indicates that it should be available, while a (?) suggests there is some doubt over it. A blank space indicates that it is most likely not an available source of influence.

The table suggests the following general conclusions:

1 Managers, Innovators and Consultants will be able to draw upon most sources of influence;
2 Trainers and Providers will have the least number of sources of influence available to them;
3 credibility, expertise, higher authority and personality are sources available to all roles;
4 rewards, sanctions and tradition are sources of influence that are the most unlikely to be available to any role, and
5 formal, positional influence is likely to be available only to the Manager.

It is one thing, of course, to know what source of influence is available to you and quite another to be able to use it effectively. As has been stressed in the description of the influence sources, care must be taken to ensure things don't work against you. Two examples will illustrate the dangers and benefits. The first concerns a Manager who had built up a good reputation (credibility) for a particular workshop programme. He had the backing of a powerful director. When that director left, his replacement was not keen on the workshop idea. The workshops were dropped and, because the Manager had little else to offer, the new director developed his own training resource. The second is about another Manager/Provider who wished to change the role of his Trainers more to that of Consultants. He did this by gaining political access at the top level (even though his own boss was not supportive) and by closing headquarters trainer offices so that his staff were forced to go out and talk to manager-clients.

To be successful in gaining influence, you must:

● know what you want;
● sell its importance to the organization (not to training);
● have confidence in what you are doing;

- carefully assess the benefits and dangers in using a particular source of influence;
- start in a small way and gain experience, and
- demonstrate the benefits and success of the new role to those who had helped you.

REMEMBER:

Organizations do things in different ways and have different values. What is acceptable behaviour in one will not be acceptable in another. An influence attempt that goes against the culture might make things worse.

SUMMARY

In this chapter we have looked at:

1   the different kinds of roles trainers can adopt ('trainer', 'provider', 'consultant', 'innovator', and 'manager');

2   the factors that influence the kind of role adopted (formal role, experience and preference, expectations and attitudes of others, organization culture, needs of the organization, chances of being successful in the role, and changing circumstances);

3   how to review your role using the Role Review Cycle (Figure 3:2) and the Role Analysis Questionnaire (Table 3:1);

4   how to gain the right experience in a new role (experimenting, working with others, job swaps, exchange of job, action learning, seminars and workshops and open learning programmes);

5   how to gain influence through your role (via formal position, tradition, rewards and sanctions, higher authority, political access, expertise, credibility, personality, access to information and resources, and coalition), and

6   how to identify the right source of influence (via Table 3:2).

We have considered some of the benefits and dangers in taking on new roles, and have stressed that there is no one best role and that what is appropriate to one situation or company may not be appropriate to others. The choice, therefore, is partly yours.

We now turn to some specific aspects of improving trainer effectiveness. The remaining chapters will concentrate on how to become more effective in particular roles and contexts, and how training as a whole needs to adapt to the organization's changing business needs.

REFERENCES/FURTHER READING

On different ways of looking at what trainers do

Those drawn upon this chapter are:

Bennett, R. and Leduchowicz, T., 'What Makes for an Effective Trainer?', *Journal of European Industrial Training Monograph*, 1983, vol. 7, no. 2, (UK).

Foo Meng Tong, 'Roles of the Trainer', *STADA Annual*, Singapore Training and Development Association, 1985.

Leduchowicz, T., 'Trainer Role and Effectiveness – A Review of Literature', *International Journal of Manpower*, 1982, vol. 3, no. 1, pp. 2–9, (UK).

McLagen, P.A., *Models for Excellence* (The Conclusions and Recommendations of the ASTD Training and Development Competancy Study), American Society for Training and Development, 1983 (USA).

Pettigrew, A.M., Jones, G.R., and Reason, P.W., *Training and Development Roles in Their Organisational Setting:* Manpower Services Commission, 1982 (UK).

Thames Valley Training, *Journal of the Thames Valley Training Association,* issue no. 6, 1985 (UK).

The classifications of Bennett and Leduchowicz, McLagan, and Pettigrew are particularly detailed and are research-based.

On power and influence

Two particularly useful sources are:

French, J.R.P., and Raven, B.H., 'The Bases of Social Power' in D. Cartwright (ed.), *Studies in Social Power,* University of Michigan Press, Michigan, 1959 (USA).

Kipnis, D., and Schmidt, S.M., *Profiles of Organisational Influence Strategies:* University Associates, 1982 San Diego (CA). (A set of questionnaires and a respondent's guide).

4 A Question of Style

David Flegg and Josephine McHale

What do you need to be an effective trainer? Judging by the criticisms delegates have been known to make, they expect their trainer to be:

- a charismatic orator (to keep the group hanging upon every word);
- an actor with flair (to keep the group entertained and wakeful, even during the languor of the post prandial session);
- a technological wizard (to revitalize failing equipment);
- an unflaggingly extrovert and sociable personality (for the late night bar sessions which are a feature of residential courses);
- an expert in everyone else's field as well as their own.

If you don't recognize yourself in these descriptors, don't despair. It might increase your end-of-course popularity ratings if you are the living embodiment of these caricatures but effective trainers are an altogether more subtle breed, with skills that are not always apparent to the uninitiated.

Effective trainers help people learn. They see things from their clients' point of view and can create conditions which encourage learning. They recognize potential barriers to learning and avoid doing things which trigger them. In other words, they have developed what we call an effective training style. Just what this means in practice is the subject of this chapter.

In our exploration of style, we are making two assumptions. The first is that you have already acquired the basic techniques of training and are comfortable in front of your course members, using the standard equipment and running various activities. The second is that you are familiar with the range of training methods open to you – role playing, simulations, case studies, group exercises etc., to name just some of your options. We will not therefore be discussing these possibilities in detail, nor be giving advice on their appropriateness in satisfying different training needs.

What we *will* be concerned with are those vitally important things you do and say in planning and implementing your training programmes – ways of putting things across to your clients, ways of helping them to learn from experience, particularly from things that have gone wrong, and developing in them an awareness of their behaviour which will help them to continue learning even when they no longer have you to guide them. We will be asking you to reflect upon the way you see yourself and your clients as participants in the learning process.

Our emphasis throughout is on the needs of the learner and on the things you can do to help him or her learn. Our comments are based on a substantial research programme on what characterizes effective trainers and instructors and on our own varied experiences of training in many different situations.

In considering the various aspects of style, we have taken as our starting point each time a typical comment about learning which might be made by a thoughtful delegate on one of your courses. We then give a brief indication of the implications for the training style you adopt, followed by a paragraph on 'Issues' which relates the comment and its implications to the interaction between the trainer and learner and their joint participation in the learning process.

A more detailed treatment of the points raised is given in the final section. This describes what you can do to prepare and run your training programmes in a way which creates the conditions which are most helpful to the learner.

We are aware that the readers of this chapter will be trainers in a wide variety of different subject areas but we hope that you will recognize that the same principles of effective style apply no matter what the content is. If you don't find an illustration which fits your subject, then try devising one of your own. That way, you will provide yourself with a context within which you can think about what we have said. If you come across suggestions which don't immediately fit in with your approach, try to resist the easy 'But it won't work with my delegates' reaction. Think carefully about each point. Try it out and if it doesn't work the first time, try again in a slightly different way. Treat yourself in the way we suggest you treat your delegates – give yourself plenty of practice and the time to reflect on what you do. By being an effective learner, you can help yourself become an effective trainer.

SETTING COURSE OBJECTIVES

Client

'I am likely to learn if a course is relevant to my work and is pitched at the right level'.

Implications for training style

Ideally, providing training programmes is the outcome of negotiation, not something which a training department imposes on its clientele. Try to find out as specifically as possible what is needed and tailor your programmes to fit. (See also 'Finding where they are on the map' page 76.)

The issues

In an ideal world, a trainer would be able to design training programmes around the specific needs of those who attend. This would ensure a close fit between the objectives of a course and its relevance to course members and remove the first potential barrier to learning. However, in reality, the assumption is made that enough people have training needs which are sufficiently similar to warrant the provision of a menu of standard courses. For most trainers, designing tailor-made courses for different groups of people will be only a small part of their work.

The implication of this for you as a trainer is that you will most probably have on your course individuals of very different backgrounds, experience and knowledge. They will be there because their boss sent them, because it is departmental policy, because they are standing in for the original nominee, or for a host of other reasons, only some of which will be related to actual need and the conviction that your course is particularly suitable for them. The problem for you is that of finding out their objectives, and of reconciling them with those you have defined for your course.

What you can do

Pre-course preparation

If you are in the position of providing standard courses, your first priority must be to give as much information as possible about:

- content, training methods and learning opportunities;
- who the course might benefit, and
- what a delegate might expect to get out of it.

You cannot guarantee that this information will get to the right people (and the person who attends is sometimes woefully ill-informed about what to expect), nor can you be sure that the information will be read. However, you will be making it easier for those who do recognize the importance of selecting suitable courses for themselves or for others, and who wish to make an informed choice.

If you are part of an in-house training function, you may be in a position to talk to those who will attend your course and to anyone else involved in the nomination. Use this opportunity wherever possible. It will enable you to draw attention to the course information that you have prepared and to discuss the relevance of the course to the individual's needs. It will also help you to prepare yourself for the course and to make amendments which might benefit your clients. The more relevant to them that you can make your training, the more likely they are to learn from it.

If you are in the position of providing public courses, you are unlikely to have spoken contact with prospective delegates. The alternative is to get them to provide some information about themselves and what they are looking for by sending them a questionnaire to be returned with their booking. This can be helpful but is rarely as informative as speaking directly to the person concerned.

On the course

The negotiation and definition of objectives is not confined to your pre-course preparation. When you come face to face with delegates on your course, you will need to consider the question of objectives again.

Faced with an unfamiliar group about whom you have little or no information, you can get the course off to a secure start by checking whether your predefined objectives are acceptable or whether there is anything else they would like to cover. (Be prepared though, to adapt your plans if necessary, in the light of what they say.)

The advantage of starting in this way is that it focuses delegates' minds on why they are there and what they want to get out of the event. This is a positive frame of mind in which to approach learning.

SIGNPOSTING WITHIN THE COURSE

Client

'I learn best when I know where I am going. It also helps if I know why we're doing something – especially as some of the exercises on management training courses are a bit weird!'

Implications for training style

Check that you keep delegates informed about what you will be asking them to do, and why.

The issues

We dwelt at length on setting course objectives. They are important to you as trainer in structuring your course and in ensuring that you make it as relevant as possible to the needs of your delegates.

However, once the course gets under way, shorter term objectives become more important. These are the signposts which will help delegates to keep track of where they are in a programme and when the different issues or topics will be covered. If they have a clear structure in their minds about how the various sessions relate to the overall objectives of the course, they will find it much easier to make sense of individual activities and presentations.

What you can do

Comments such as 'We'll spend the next hour on an exercise to reinforce what we covered this morning, then after the teabreak, we will have a general discussion about where we've got to so far' are particularly useful as signposts. They provide delegates with an up-to-date plan for a specific period of time and are particularly necessary if you have deviated from your original schedule.

Be prepared to give such signposting at regular intervals, since there is no guarantee that delegates will attend to you the first time, nor that what you say will be remembered.

It will help your delegates even more if you back up your statement of *what* you are going to do, with an explanation of *why* you are going to do it. The structure of your course and the rationale behind each activity may be crystal clear to you since you have spent time planning it, but it might be less clear to course members.

Bear in mind that many people who attend training courses will have very limited experience of what is involved. Role playing, group exercises and simulations, for example, may be unfamiliar to them, leaving them uncertain of the purpose of such activities and confused about the behaviour that is expected of them. Uncertainty can lead to frustration and frustration to antagonism or withdrawal, either of which will create tension in you and in other delegates. So be generous in your explanations of what you intend doing, the reasons why you are going to do it and what delegates are likely to get out of it. This way, you will have defined some boundaries for them and created an atmosphere in which they are likely to have a go. You will have removed a potentially powerful barrier to learning and opened up the possibility that learning will result.

FINDING WHERE THEY ARE ON THE MAP

Client

'I switch off when I'm told what I know already. I went on a supervisory course recently – a new look at supervisors in our industry and aimed at people like me who had been in the job a year or two. Well – that's what it said. All it was was a rehash of the same old things that we had all worked out for ourselves long ago. I wasn't the only one who was fed up by the end of it, I can tell you.'

Implications for training style

Find out as much as you can both before a course and when the course convenes, about delegates' experience and level of knowledge. Be prepared to adapt your programme at short notice if necessary.

Issues

If delegates feel that you have misjudged the level of training that they need, and have planned a course which is either too basic or too advanced, they will quickly become frustrated and resentful. It may then be very difficult for you to retrieve the situation and recreate a climate in which they can learn.

What you can do

The message is that if you don't know where your course members are starting from, you could find it very difficult to help them find their way forward. It means that as well as finding out what they expect from your course (which helps you define the course objectives), you will also need to establish just what knowledge, experience, skills and attitudes they have in areas relevant to the content that you plan. This will enable you to check that you have pitched the course at the right level and to make adjustments if you find that you haven't.

You can get the information you want in the same way as you found out about delegates' objectives both before the course, by asking them directly or by getting them to complete a questionnaire, and during the course, by asking them about themselves in an introductory session.

Ask questions such as:

'Have you had to do anything like this before? How often?'
'How did it go? How did you feel about it?'
'Were there any particular problems?'
'What did you find easiest?'

You might also include activities which you design to get more precise information about your group and to enable you to choose a suitable place to start. (See below for examples.)

Again, be prepared to alter your plans slightly if the feedback you get warrants it. Your credibility as a trainer will be damaged if you ask for information and then fail to act on it.

If you misjudge your audience, it is likely that:

1   delegates will become angry and frustrated;
2   those who may have been sceptical about the value of training will have their prejudices confirmed;
3   there will be little learning, and
4   your reputation will suffer.

The advantages of activities illustrated in the examples are:

1   you have a clear idea of participants' state of knowledge and expertise;
2   you find out whether they have any particular confusions or misconceptions;
3   by taking the outcomes into account, you avoid unnecessary repetitions of what they already know or can do;
4   members of the group begin to interact with one another;
5   they find others are at a similar stage to themselves, and
6   the task focuses their attention on the gaps in their knowledge and therefore puts them in the right frame of mind to start learning.

Doing the sort of preliminary assessments that we have described is not always easy and it might take some ingenuity on your part to devise suitable ways. However, it is worth the effort, so long as you can do it without making course members feel threatened, or that they are back in a school classroom being tested by a teacher.

It is worth reiterating here that your pre-course information should be as detailed and specific as possible so that you minimize the risk of people making an unsuitable choice in relation to their own level of experience.

Examples of activities

Course title: An introduction to computing

Target audience: Managers who will have to use computers in the course of their job but who as yet have had no specific training in their use nor in the potential benefits.

Problem: The course assumes no knowledge, thus indicating that you are willing to start from scratch. However, many people will have picked up some knowledge about computer terminology, if only through helping their children to load computer games.

You know from past experience that knowledge picked up in this way is often incomplete and sometimes inexact. If the course is to make sense, it must be built on secure foundations, so some form of activity is necessary to ensure that delegates do not get left behind.

A solution: You devise a quiz which tests knowledge of basic terminology and understanding of computing systems. You ask delegates to work through this in pairs. When they have finished, you take each item separately and invite the group to supply you with the answer. If any small confusions emerge, you can deal with them in passing. If more radical treatment is needed, you can devote more time to the problem a little later. In either case, you have got the information about your group which will enable you to decide exactly where you need to start.

Course title: Equal opportunities interviewing

Target audience: Personnel managers responsible for recruitment and selection: line managers who are involved in the selection process.

Problem: Many people are not fully aware of the biased attitudes which can influence their judgement. You feel that your course will not have the impact you are looking for unless different attitudes and points of view are brought out into the open.

A solution: You ask course members to divide themselves into small groups, to discuss a case study relating to equal opportunities and to reach a consensus about what should have been done in the situation described. In this way, a wide range of issues are aired, and debated. Because of their involvement in the discussion, participants are more likely to have thought about what was involved than if they had merely listened to a presentation on the same subject by you.

Course title: Customer contact skills

Target Audience: Counter staff in a travel agency;

Problem: The staff attending your course have all worked in an agency for at least a year. It is company policy that they receive periodic refresher training, partly to become familiar with new company services and partly to brush up their sales techniques. You need to find out what sort of coaching they require so that you avoid the possibility of alienating them by teaching them things they already know.

A solution: You ask them some very specific questions which require them to answer as though they were on the job. For example:

- What would you say to a customer who complained that she had been rudely treated on a recent flight?
- What would you say to a customer who looked unhappy when told his flight had been changed from Heathrow to Gatwick?
- How would you respond to a customer who got angry when you explained that he could not change the date of his booking?

From the answers you get to questions such as these, you would be able to judge where it would be appropriate to start with that particular group.

AVOIDING OVERLOAD

Client

'There have been many times on courses when I have wanted to creep into a corner and sort things out in my own mind before I'm ready to take in anything more.'

Implications for training style

Recognize that delegates will not be able to take in a lot of information without having time to consolidate it. Avoid overloading them. Involve them in doing or thinking about something as often as possible, and keep the amount of time they merely watch and listen to a minimum.

The issues

'Information overload' is a common condition on courses, and is particularly likely to happen when:

1   a lot of new information is being put across;
2   complex concepts are presented;
3   a presentation is lengthy;
4   all the information comes from the same source;
5   learners are not given an opportunity to consolidate, or question the input;
6   learners are not given the opportunity to try something out for themselves and
7   learners are not allowed sufficient time to reflect upon something they have just experienced.

Some of the occasions when you might indavertently put your course members in these situations are when:

1   you want to communicate your knowledge and enthusiasm for your subject, so your presentations go on just that little bit too long;
2   you spot so many things to comment on when you see a novice learning a skill that well meant advice pours out of you;

3   you feel you are in the ideal position to give unbiased feedback on group activities and exercises and so your comments dominate the debriefing sessions, and

4   you feel that since you are the trainer, you are the one that delegates have come to learn from and that it is up to you to provide the knowledge, the insights and the connections as well as the blueprint for future improvements.

The danger is that though you may be striving to be as helpful as you can and acting with the best of intentions, you could be causing problems for your delegates. You risk overwhelming them.

The temptations are all too real, but to fall prey to them is to ignore some very fundamental aspects of the learning process.

The most significant of these is that our attention span is very limited. The amount we can learn from what other people tell us is therefore restricted by how much we can take in. If we are to absorb new information, we need ample opportunity to process it and to integrate it with what we already know. We also need to try things out in practice and think through the results.

What you can do

The key to avoiding overload is to do everything you can to involve the learner in some way. What this will mean in practice will depend on the situation. We have selected some of the most common danger points and have commented on them below. We have supplemented this with additional points where appropriate.

Putting across information in presentations

There are bound to be times when the most appropriate way for you to get your course members to learn about something is to tell them. The danger about this method is that it is easy for you to end up doing all the work while your audience sit passively listening.

If they are to learn from what you say, it is important that their minds are kept active, so that they fit the new information into a framework and relate it to what they already know. The problem is that it is difficult to do this if at the same time they have to continue listening to you. Fortunately, there are many things that you can do to help them and to ensure that your presentations are effective.

Your starting point is making your presentation as clearly structured and memorable as you can. Some ways of doing this are listed below.

- Structure your talk very carefully. Make the structure obvious by writing it up on your flip chart and explaining it to your group. You can give them extra help by referring back to your original plan where appropriate and indicating the point you have reached. By doing this, you will give each participant a framework which will help them keep track of where you have got to in your presentation. It's another way of providing the short-term signposts that we discussed earlier.

- Display on the OHP, the essential points of each part of your presentation. Reveal them one by one as you get to them. Do not make the mistake of writing out a detailed account of what you are saying and then reading aloud from this.

- Provide whatever additional visual aids you think will be helpful. If they are colourful and humorous, so much the better.

- Illustrate your points with examples. This brings the theory down to earth. Again, the addition of humour will help to make things stick.

- Give explanations for the things you say. This helps to increase the level of understanding that your audience will achieve.

- Give verbal summaries of what you have covered, after each part of your presentation.

- Provide handouts which summarize your main points.

Once you are confident that you have got your contribution sorted out to your satisfaction, consider next how you can involve your audience. Their learning will be greatest if you can break up your input by giving them something to do themselves, or by asking them questions where you can without distracting them from your overall framework. This means that they will be more actively involved than if they were merely sitting and listening.

Giving instructions

The start of an exercise is typically a time of considerable confusion with delegates trying to arrange their groups, listen to instructions, work out tactics etc. all at the same time. They may even still be mulling over what has gone immediately before. Your explanation of what you would like them to do, and what you expect them to get out of an activity, may be too much for them to take in at that moment.

You can minimize the likelihood of overload by:

1   ensuring that the group has had ample time to consider what has gone before and are therefore likely to be able to give you their attention;
2   keeping your instructions brief and clear, and
3   reducing the load on delegates' memories by providing a written version of the instructions, either as a handout or else displayed on an OHP while the activity gets under way.

Answering questions

Many of the questions that delegates ask will be on topics with which you are very familiar. They may also touch on issues which are important to you. The temptation then is to give a detailed and wide ranging response which covers too many points for the questioner to take in and which may not be appropriate at that particular point in your training programme.

You can avoid overloading delegates in this way by:

1   keeping your reply very short;
2   inviting the questioner to discuss it with you at the next break when you would have more time to do it justice without the risk of losing the attention of other delegates;
3   opening up the question to the group for discussion, if the issue is sufficiently important and of general interest; and
4   assuring the questioner that the question is an interesting one but that you will be covering it in a later session.

It sometimes happens that a question represents a point of view at odds with the one you hold or have already put forward. If this is the case, accept that you are unlikely to convert the questioner in the space of a minute or two. Acknowledge the difference of opinion and avoid a confrontation by deferring discussion to another time. An informal chat over a pint in the bar might be the best place to talk things through.

Putting across new procedures and skills

There will be many occasions when you will be training people in a new skill or procedure. The possibilities are endless but whether you are teaching a school leaver to operate a computer or a senior manager to conduct an appraisal interview, there is one fundamental point that all such training sessions have in common: the rapidity with which learners can become overwhelmed by all the new things that they have to do. As soon as it is practical to do so (safety considerations may sometimes dictate when this is), let the learner have a go at doing something. Don't expect them merely to watch and/or listen for anything more than short periods of time. They may be able to find out in a few minutes of direct experience what could take you far longer to explain.

The implications for learning go beyond this, though. By enabling learners to put theory into practice, or to discover things for themselves, the load on their memory is much less than if they were trying to remember what you had said. The risk of overloading is therefore considerably reduced, and the likelihood of learning is enormously increased.

Debriefing and giving feedback

The possibility of giving delegates more information than they can cope with is particularly strong at the end of an exercise or activity, when you want them to learn from what they have experienced. It is natural and understandable that you, from your unique vantage point of experienced observer, want to share with the participants all your insights into what you saw happening. Before you do so, though, think about what the outcome might be.

If the exercise has been a substantial one in terms of time and commitment from delegates, each participant will have his or her own feelings about what they have just been through as individuals and as a group. Whatever their state of mind – be it elated, downcast, frustrated or excited – it is unlikely that they will be willing to sit down and listen attentively to your version of what happened. They are likely to become overloaded very quickly, since there will be so many other thoughts in their mind at the time, and they will soon cease to take in what you are saying.

In situations like this, as with so many others on training

courses, delegates need time to reflect, to think and to consolidate. They do not want additional input and will probably not be able to cope with it. The most effective thing you can do initially is to let them do the talking. Your main contribution will be to help them structure their thoughts and to explore the implications of what they have experienced. Passing on your insights might be confined to filling in some gaps in their awareness.

Having said that, we would stress that it is only a guideline, and there may be situations where your judgement leads you into a different course of action. For example, the need to provide some very specific feedback to an individual at an early stage of learning a skill may warrant you doing more of the talking. The danger of overload still applies, though, so keep your input short and to the point.

At this point, we simply wish to make you aware of the possibility of overloading your delegates when it comes to giving them feedback. In 'Developing the habit of self-assessment' and 'What to do when things go wrong', we will discuss in more detail how you can help them learn from their experiences.

CREATING THE RIGHT ATMOSPHERE

Client

'I'm not very happy about taking part in exercises and such like if I think I'm going to end up feeling a fool.'

Implications for training style

If you want people to learn from the various activities and exercises that you think are helpful, you have to create a friendly and supportive atmosphere which encourages delegates to feel safe and creates an environment in which they feel willing to try things out.

Issues

Learning involves change – in attitudes, in long established habits, in ways of thinking – and change involves risk. If delegates are to be willing to expose themselves to risk, they need to feel that whatever they do and say, they will not be put down or made to feel foolish. If delegates feel vulnerable, their willingness to experiment will be inhibited and the likelihood of learning will be reduced.

What you can do

A training course can be a stressful experience for some delegates. Exercises and activities which expose individuals' behaviour and reactions to public scrutiny can be especially threatening. Your efforts to create a friendly and supportive environment must therefore start right at the beginning of the course and set the tone for its duration.

Once you and the delegates have introduced yourselves to each other, it is well worth your while spending a few minutes setting the scene for what will follow. If you explain briefly how people learn and how you have taken account of this in your course design, you will help delegates to understand why they are asked to do certain things and how they might expect to benefit.

You will be giving further reassurance to those who might need it if you also stress that each one of them has the right not to participate in something if he or she so chooses. There will be few occasions when a delegate will exercise this right, but it is important to an individual's sense of self control that they retain the option to opt out if necessary. Freedom of choice is an important prerequisite to learning. Coercion has a depressing effect. If necessary, reiterate the option during your course to emphasize that you meant what you said in your introduction.

You can make apparent your respect for the individual, and thereby help to create the right atmosphere, through the way you interact with each course member. Below are just some of the ways in which you can build up their trust in you:

1   Deal with each question courteously, no matter how many times you have had to answer it in the past.

2   If you don't know the answer to a question, say so calmly and non-defensively. Admit your limitations.

3   Don't jump to conclusions about what delegates are saying simply because it sounds similar to what you have heard before.

4   Invite comments from delegates, instead of always giving your comments first.

5   Be prepared to disclose things about yourself if you are expecting delegates to do this.

6   Be factual in your comments, not evaluative: (e.g. 'You asked a lot of closed questions' is more acceptable and useful than 'Your questions were poor').

7   Avoid activities which are designed to catch people out – you
    will lose their trust and make them suspicious of everything
    else you do.
8   Be honest about yourself.
9   Be open and honest to delegates about what you want them to
    do and why.

CHECKING UNDERSTANDING

Client

'There were lots of things along the way that we hadn't quite got the
hang of, but the trainer didn't give us a chance to sort them
out.'

Implications for training style

Your familiarity with your subject matter may lead you to
overestimate the rate at which delegates can absorb things. You
therefore need to make it easy for them to raise queries or
uncertainties. You also need to keep a check on their progress so
that you can adjust your plans to accommodate their needs.

Issues

If delegates are to be active participants in the learning process, it
is important that they should be able to ask questions, express
doubts or articulate problems. This way, they are helping
themselves to consolidate what they are learning and to integrate it
into what they already know.

   Where the content of a course is such that mastery of one topic
is a prerequisite to moving on to another, it is also vital for the
trainer to check whether or not delegates have attained that
mastery and whether it is therefore appropriate to go ahead with
new inputs. Failure to grasp the fundamentals would make it
difficult for delegates to learn from what came later.

What you can do

Your starting point is to make it clear in your introduction to the
course that learning involves two way communication, not just
one way from you to the delegates. Emphasize that you want

delegates to raise anything they are not sure of or want further clarification on.

You can reinforce your message with questions such as:

'Is there anything you want to ask before we start the next session?'
'Is that clear or would you like to go through anything again?'
'Any questions so far?'
'OK so far? Sure?'

In each case, follow your question with a pause long enough to make it clear that you really are inviting people to speak.

Checking in the general way suggested above gives delegates an opportunity to seek clarification. For you, though, it will provide only a limited amount of information about the stage your group has reached, since there will always be those who prefer to struggle on without admitting their difficulties. Where it is important for you to know exactly how individuals are progressing, you will need to check more specifically.

You may already be familiar with one standard way of doing this, namely:

POSE: PAUSE: POUNCE:

The trainer poses a question, pauses to give everyone time to consider the answer and then asks a particular person to give a reply. If an answer is not forthcoming, the trainer moves on to someone else. If this can be done without threat and without embarrassing those who fail to answer, then this is a possible way of making specific checks on what delegates have absorbed. It does, however, have drawbacks:

1   it can make you sound like a school teacher, which is not desirable on a training course;
2   you only find out what the respondent to each question knows, not the group as a whole, and
3   it is often possible to answer a question with appropriate key words and phrases, without fully understanding the concepts.

An alternative which might be more satisfactory, is to set tasks which involve the application of knowledge. Working in pairs or small groups, or as one big group led by you, completion of the task will help individuals recognize the extent to which they have grasped a subject and enable them to fill in the gaps in their knowledge. You will get to know the level of understanding they have reached by observing and listening to each group in turn as they work through the activity, from the questions they ask you and from the standard they achieve on the task. Thus you get the information you need and course members are actively involved in a useful piece of revision.

An additional benefit is that it serves a diagnostic purpose. It enables you to evaluate the effectiveness of separate parts of your training programme and will help you to identify those parts which may need revising.

Examples of ways in which this could be done

Course: Accounting for managers:
Test the group's understanding of basic accounting procedures by giving them a completed balance sheet to study and questions to answer on the basis of information contained on it.

Course: An introduction to marketing:
Test the group's understanding of marketing plans by providing an example of one already compiled and ask them to comment on what is satisfactory or unsatisfactory about it.

Course: Developing interviewing skills:
To find out whether the group is ready to try role playing exercises, test their understanding of the different ways of asking questions by asking them to watch a video recording of an interview and ask them to comment on how the interviewer asked questions.

DEVELOPING THE HABIT OF SELF-ASSESSMENT

Client

'The trainer kept making us think for ourselves about what we did – I found that a very useful way of learning.'

Implications for training style

It is in the delegates' interests to encourage them to develop the habit of assessing their own performance rather than letting them rely on other people (particularly you, on a training course) to do it for them. This means that an important aspect of effective training style is the ability to know when to hold back your own opinions and to adopt a questioning technique which elicits opinions from delegates.

Issues

You may sometimes be confronted with delegates whose attitude is 'You are the trainer; you tell me what to do . . . how to react . . . how well I did . . .'. You may want to provide this sort of information anyway. But if learning is to be a process which can happen at any time and in any situation, it is ultimately the responsibility of the learner. We all have to become our own observers and trainers.

A training course, under the guidance of an effective trainer, is an opportunity for participants to acquire or to reinforce the habit of looking critically at themselves, at what they do and how they do it, and to assess what improvements may be necessary. If you take this responsibility away from delegates by providing all the information yourself, you will be encouraging them to rely on your judgement instead of developing their own. This means that when they no longer have your guidance, their learning might be less effective than it could otherwise be.

What you can do

Try to think yourself into the role of helper and facilitator rather than 'teller'. There will of course be many occasions when it is entirely appropriate for you to be the source of information for your course members. Equally, there may be more opportunities than you have hitherto realized to get them working things out for themselves.

A useful starting point at the end of any exercise is a general question such as 'How did that feel?' or 'How do you think it went that time?' Follow this up with more specific questions, encouraging delegates to review their experience systematically by identifying what they want to consider and then working through the categories one at a time. It is worth remembering that what you would like them to concentrate on might not always be so important to the group nor can you always be aware of which aspects of performance cause them most concern, so give each individual plenty of opportunity to voice their reactions. You can always add your comments later if you find that they have not already been covered.

Don't allow delegates to stop at general statements like 'It was a lot better' or 'I think I was hopeless'. Ask for specific examples which illustrate their judgement otherwise your discussion with them might be based on very different perceptions of what they meant.

Encourage them to compare one experience with another and to explore the differences. This can be a powerful technique for understanding why different things happen in different situations whether it is done by one person looking at their own performance or by the group commenting on each other. For example:

'Why do you think your second presentation was so much better than your first? What were you doing differently?'

'What extra information did the interviewer elicit the second time round? What had changed? Why?'

Making such comparisons helps you to answer the question 'why?', which is at the heart of self-assessment.

WHAT TO DO WHEN THINGS GO WRONG

Client

'It's often said that we learn from our mistakes. But if that's the case, why do the same things go wrong again and again?'

Implications for training style

In most types of training, mistakes are inevitable, but learning from them sometimes needs careful management. Merely to accept that something has gone wrong will not necessarily ensure that it won't happen again. An analysis of why it happened is likely to be much more helpful, coupled with a conscious decision about what to do differently to prevent its repetition.

If you can help delegates to work this out for themselves, the message will be much more acceptable and it is more likely to result in change.

Issues

An important issue here is again encouraging delegates to adopt the habit of reviewing themselves, so that they avoid becoming reliant on someone else to point out where they are going wrong. This way, learning is more likely to continue beyond the training course.

What you can do

Ask course members to identify where things went off the rails in an exercise and why they think this happened. If you have already provided them with examples of good practice (a well structured and presented report, or a video of an effective presentation, for example, or whatever models are appropriate to your course), they can compare their own performance with them and ask themselves 'what did I do differently? What effect did it have on the final outcome?'

It is important that delegates have the opportunity to do this, because:

1   it reinforces the self-reviewing habit;
2   it reduces the defensiveness that sometimes arises in reaction to feedback about what went wrong, however tactfully this is put;
3   it enables you to judge how far they have developed in their awareness of what they did and what they might have done, allowing you to adjust the emphasis of subsequent sessions if necessary, and
4   once delegates have acquired some familiarity with what they are doing, they usually have a good idea of what went wrong, and their ability to see this deserves acknowledgement.

If, however, you find that things have gone wrong without delegates being aware of them, then proceed carefully or you could have a rebellion on your hands! One possible way of handling the situation is to focus their attention on a particular aspect of the exercise.

For example 'Let's look at the way the group allocated tasks amongst themselves at the beginning.' Ask the group to describe what happened and how they felt about it, then invite them to discuss whether there were any other ways in which they might have approached things.

If nothing is forthcoming at this stage, you have various options:

1   To tell them what you saw and what you think might have been better. This should be acceptable to a confident group

with whom you have built up a good relationship. If the group has not reached this stage, you must tread carefully. There is a strong possibility that the group will react defensively and present you with all sorts of arguments as to why your proposals would not have worked, especially if they are under the illusion that things went fairly well. Once these barriers go up, any further learning is unlikely until you have re-established your credibility and trust with the group.

2   To accept that the group is not yet ready to tackle the issues. If so, drop the issue for the time being and come back to it later. In the meantime, you will probably have to do some more preliminary work to get the group to the stage of development that you want, so it will pay you to have contingency plans up your sleeve to cope with this possibility.

3   To round off the discussion when you find that the group has nothing more to say, and then set another exercise which will illuminate the issues of which they had hitherto been unaware. This does demand flexibility and resourcefulness on the part of the trainer, but it has the advantage of involving the participants in discovering for themselves the shortfalls in their own performance. Since each individual can be his own best critic, this self-discovery is often far more powerful than receiving criticism from someone else.

It is especially important that you establish the right sort of atmosphere when dealing with a performance which is below par, so that the delegates see these occasions as an opportunity to learn something. Remind delegates that the training course is a safe place in which to try out things which would not be possible on the job, and that learning can be enriched if they are willing to take risks. Try to prevent the tone of the discussion from becoming too negative by balancing criticisms (even self-criticisms) with things which went well.

If delegates find that things didn't work out as they had wished in the course of an exercise, and have identified what went wrong and why, it is important to complete the process of learning from such situations by working through two further stages.

The first, to which we referred earlier, is to ensure that delegates know what to do to prevent things going wrong in the same way again. This means that debriefing sessions must cover exactly what is required to improve performance the next time round.

For example, it is not enough to say that a delegate should try to put an interviewee more at ease. The specific behaviours which will help this to happen, such as smiling more, maintaining eye contact, nodding sympathetically, must be spelled out. Allow time for participants to come up with their own alternatives. They may well supplement your own suggestions.

The final stage is to provide the means for delegates to practise the new behaviours. One simulated interview on an 'Interviewing skills' course will highlight some problems to work on but two or more further interviews will be necessary if new skills are to be developed. If your course objectives are concerned with the acquisition of skill, then the more practice and feedback sessions that you can provide, the better.

PARTING SHOTS

In talking about effective training style, we have emphasized the importance of involving delegates, of keeping them mentally alert and of helping them work things out for themselves. We say this in the firm belief, backed up by applied research, that these principles help to create the conditions which are most favourable to learning.

However, in encouraging you to see yourself as a 'helper' or facilitator rather than a 'teller', we may have left you with the impression that the less you say, the more effective you will be. This is not the case. We are not advocating that you adopt wholesale the approach of 'let them work it all out for themselves'. It would clearly be unwise to ask them to spend 30 minutes discovering some obscure fact that you could have told them in three! On the other hand, there will be many occasions when a few minutes practical experience will mean more to them than all the talking you can do.

So what we do advocate is that you seek a balance between telling them things and getting them to work things out for themselves. To give you a rough idea of the proportions that we think are effective, try asking for one bit of information for every three or so that you put across. Treat this ratio as a very crude guide, though, and use it with discretion.

Achieving the right balance is half the battle. If you combine this with the application of the other principles we have described, you will be well on the road to becoming effective as a trainer. From then on, it's a matter of practice and fine tuning.

The key points emerging from this Chapter are summarized in Table 4:1. Use it as a checklist for assessing how effective you are in the Trainer (i.e. Instructing) role. How many of the nine points can you claim to meet? How would your colleagues and trainees rate? The checklist also provides useful tips on what you can do about each point.

Further reading is then provided for those who wish to explore more deeply and broadly.

Table 4:1
Summary of factors influencing learning, and of key actions

Learning is most likely when:	*What the trainer can do:*
The course is relevant to learners' needs and pitched at right level	Give as much pre-course information as possible; find out what delegates want
Learners know where they are going and why	Give short-term signposts
The trainer acknowledges delegates' levels of knowledge and experience	Find out as much as you can about where delegates are starting from
The learner has time to digest information before more is given	Avoid overloading the learner; build in time for consolidation; use aids (handouts, OHPs, summaries etc.) to reduce memory load
The learner feels secure and un-threatened	Create the right sort of atmosphere by being friendly, non-evaluative, honest and supportive
The learner can cope with the pace of teaching	Regularly check the level of understanding and encourage learners to raise queries, doubts, problems etc.
Learners take responsibility for their own learning	Encourage learners to adopt the habit of self-assessment; don't let them get dependent on you
Mistakes are made and are dealt with helpfully	Establish what went wrong and why and how to prevent it happening again; be non-evaluative in your feedback
The learner is involved in the learning process	Adopt the role of 'helper' rather than teller

FURTHER READING

This chapter has concentrated on effective training style – what trainers say and do to help people learn. Some of the research from which this focus originated is described in:

Newsham, D., *What's in a Style?*, Industrial Training Research Unit, Lloyds Bank Chambers, Hobson Street, Cambridge, 1975 9pp.

An objective method of analysing the strengths and weaknesses of instructional style is described in the following article:

Flegg, D.W., 'Developing Instructors to meet Training Needs', *Personnel Management*, May, 1983.

The authors have also written distance learning materials, with audio-cassette support material. The content of the module is similar to that of this chapter, but the emphasis is on its application to on-the-job training, with numerous practical exercises to help readers relate the points to their own work.

McHale, J. and Flegg, D.W., *Putting it across: The OPTIS Guide to Effective Instruction*. OPTIS, Gosford Hill School, Oxford Road, Kidlington, Oxford. OX5 2NT.

Although style has been identified in research as being the most significant factor in determining the success of training, there are obviously many other things for the trainer to consider. The following books may be useful to complete the contents of this chapter:

Binsted, D., Developments in Interpersonal Skills Training, Gower, Aldershot 1986, 220pp.

Eitington, J.E., *The Winning Trainer*, Gulf, Houston 1984.

Loughary, J.W., and Hopson, B., *Producing Workshops, Seminars and Short Courses – A Trainer's Handbook*, Follet Publishing Co., 1976.

Rae, L., *The Skills of Human Relations Training: A guide for managers and practitioners*, Gower, Aldershot 1985, 278pp.

Rae, L., *The Skills of Training: A guide for managers and practitioners*, Gower, Aldershot 1983, 208pp.

Phillips, K., and Fraser, T. *The Management of Interpersonal Skills Training*, Gower, Aldershot 1982, 240pp.

5 The Skills of Change-making

Alun Jones

Training is changing. Traditionally the task of the training officer has been to provide training for the organization. The 'provisions' have taken the form of training programmes and courses which in their turn have provided the skilled people the organization required. This will continue to be an important task for trainers, especially as changes in technology and markets demand rapid changes in skills.

But training itself is experiencing massive changes. Not only in its own technology and methodology but in the contribution it can make to organizations which have to change. In recent years more and more trainers have become involved in tasks inside the departments of their organizations which complement and supplement their traditional tasks inside their training schools, colleges and departments. They are becoming more intimately concerned with how the organization works, with its structures, processes and relationships, as well as with helping its individuals to learn.

Their interest is how the whole organization changes and learns, and learns to change in aggregate, as opposed simply to how discrete individuals learn to change. Their focus has become the organization as a whole rather than the separate individuals who work in it. They are evolving from trainer–teachers into trainer–consultants. Chapter 3 has described the shifts in these roles. This chapter deals with the new skills and other learning needs which the trainers themselves will have to acquire and satisfy in order to fulfil a more interventionist role.

INTERVENTIONS FOR TRAINERS

If trainers are to help their organization change by being more directly interventionist then two requirements are essential:

1   for trainers to develop a more strategic and organizational view of their training activities: this will require trainers to extend their own boundaries of time and space, and
2   for trainers to become more aware of, and then to develop, the training skills which have greatest effect in intervening and penetrating usefully into their organization when it is learning how to change.

Training interventions – definitions

A Theory of Intervention has been built up over the past 10–15 years based on the behavioural sciences and the growing theory of organizations.

Trainers have borrowed the term 'intervention' from these academic and practising behavioural scientists, many of whom are involved in Organizational Development (OD) as opposed to training in the traditional sense. It would, therefore, be well to explore the use and implications of the term for trainers.

Boundaries

The clearest way to tackle the idea of intervention is from the point of view of boundaries. To intervene implies penetrating and 'getting into', i.e. crossing the other's boundary. Trainers normally intervene across an individual's boundary. If they are to become more interventionist in organizational terms it follows that they need to seek ways of crossing organizational boundaries; but conversely they have to be allowed to cross these boundaries by line-managers. And once across them they have to be able to demonstrate both ability and value. Further, crossing boundaries into probably unknown territory is often a much more risky business than staying where you are.

Action

Secondly, intervention implies getting something to happen.

Often trainers' activities have concentrated on bringing about learning. The criticism has been that the learning has not resulted in either actions or results in the organization. Too often it has been intellectual, theoretical and 'head-level' learning only.

Often, because learning and action have been separated by concentrating learning only in the 'classroom', the interventions of the trainers have sometimes made action 'out there' even more difficult, rather than enabling it to happen. Compare the frustration and resulting lowering of morale and motivation when staff return from training courses with new skills and ideas they are not allowed to apply or develop further. So successful interventions have an expectation of action and results – things must happen in the organization because of them.

Goals

Thirdly, the action resulting from the intervention is purposeful. It is not any unspecified change that is the goal; it is planned and specific : a part of the organization's strategy for change.

Many trainers' goals are concerned with individuals. Often in many large organizations these goals are set mainly with a view to promotion or individual progression. Where performance has been included it is often of a personal nature, i.e. it tackles the individual's contribution only and says nothing about the organizations' structures, systems and practices which so often are the most significant limitation to improved performance. If training is to intervene in the organization itself then it follows that it must become concerned with, and involved in, meeting organizational goals and priorities.

Training specialism as intervention

Finally, any intervention is constrained by the expertise and the goals of the interventionists themselves. The concept of 'preferential specialism' is well known, i.e. specialists will find a problem in the organization which allows them to use their 'special' skills. Thus it will not be surprising that interventions from a trainer's view will reveal a particular training emphasis and expertise. And so they should if trainers have any kind of worthwhile expertise to offer. But as the emphasis moves from training as an activity the *trainer* carries out, onto *learning* inside the organization which trainees achieve, a number of new doors for more effective interventions are opened.

A working definition of Training Interventions might be:

Activities which help bring about the learning required to enable the organization solve its problems, meet its goals and change itself effectively.

But of course trainers' interventions will be constrained both by the roles offered to them by the organization and their ability to develop those roles and increase their contribution.

Thus the definition of a skilled Training Interventionist might be:

A Trainer who continually can exploit the opportunity to bring about the learning required to enable the organization solve its problems, meet its goals and change itself effectively.

The second part of this chapter identifies the skills such an interventionist will need in order to become more effective in helping organizations change.

INTERVENTION SKILLS FOR TRAINERS

Background

From a study of the experience of trainers who have been developing a more interventionist role it is possible to put together a process or cycle which describes the particular activities and skills trainers can contribute to organizations to help them change.

The activities can be grouped in a 'cycle' (Figure 5:1) under clearly defined areas, although in practice they are neither as neatly grouped nor as chronologically tidy as the list might suggest. They are an extension of the well-known training cycle to which a number of new and crucial activities have been added.

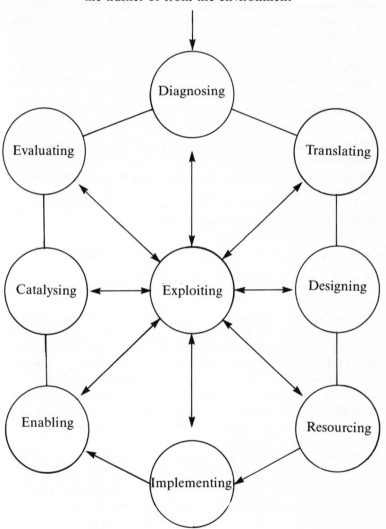

Figure 5:1 The intervention cycle

These eight categories form a cycle of Training Interventions which take the trainer more and more outside the traditional boundaries of 'training'. Like any cycle it can be entered at any point, and so the trainer's ability to use and develop whatever opportunity is offered as a chance to initiate an effective training intervention applies at all points of the cycle. Usually the cycle begins as the result of some kind of stimulus, either from outside or inside the organization. Sometimes trainers will provide the stimulus, to heighten the awareness of a real need, but they will be on dangerous ground if they merely manipulate the organization to want their 'solution'. Logically, wherever the cycle starts, the trainer will get round to helping to diagnose the need appropriately and as comprehensively as possible. So this Training Intervention Process can act as a guide to the trainer to ensure that activities are aggressively interventionist and likely to penetrate the organization. For it is 'inside' the organization and its processes that the trainer needs to contribute if training activities are to become increasingly effective in bringing about change.

Helping to diagnose the need : DIAGNOSING

Traditionally trainers have identified training needs by collecting relevant data, interpreting the data themselves and coming up with training solutions and recommendations. Very often, because the trainers have been operating largely on their own from a training framework and standpoint, the identification of training has resulted in training solutions that have not made an extensive intervention into the organization's performance problems.

In one way, Identifying Training Needs has been a harmful activity, tending towards 'separating' training needs and the subsequent training solutions from the organization's main stream of work and performance.

If a more interventionist stance is taken, the skills in this category are much more about enabling managers and staff to collect, consider and interpret valid data for themselves and the trainer's skill is to help them to do this effectively. Trainers will *add* a specialist view and a special expertise and understanding of how *learning happens,* to enable the organization to make a more comprehensive diagnosis of its problems.

Skills in taking part in and leading discussions between managers and their staff become key. Skills of listening, drawing-out information, clarifying and summarizing are crucial in this process.

Trainers may well have to provide models and suggest appropriate techniques to analyse problems or to identify organizational and business weaknesses, or at least they will need to know how they can be provided, sometimes from other specialists in the organization.

Many modern data-collection techniques involve the use of computers. Knowledge of the potential of a much more sophisticated collection and analysis of data is an important contribution the trainer can make and many Training Audits are now computer-assisted.

Determining the specific contribution of training : TRANSLATING

Trainers are not merely 'general practitioners' in the organization's diagnostic processes. They also have specialist skills and expertise to offer in their own right; but the trainer's skills in helping to diagnose the organization's needs are different in kind from skills of other specialists. They need to be able to offer the special expertise to L-I-N-K organizational needs with learning needs and objectives. To do this they must not only be skilled in determining learning objectives (an emphasis in most training courses for trainers) but equally must be able to understand the need from the organization's, and therefore the manager's, viewpoint. This is a *translating* skill, demanding fluency in both languages; training and organization. If trainers are locked too firmly into training technology and training terminology, it can be difficult for them really to listen, understand and identify themselves with the organization's needs. This is not to say that the more traditional trainer skills of job and skills and task analyses are no longer required. They undoubtedly will be important in a number of situations, but to do this linking well trainers will also need to have a good understanding of how organizations work as human and technical systems, as well as appreciating how their own particular organization works. Added to this they will need the sensitivity and skill to 'feel out' what is happening in the organization and to translate this into relevant learning needs.

The ability to present this data clearly and convincingly in writing will often be crucial. These 'linking' skills would seem to be a critical factor in determining how effectively training contributes to the mainstream of business and organizational activity and performance. It is probably what has most often been missing and its absence has been one of the causes of training and trainers remaining in a peripheral and sometimes inconsequential position *vis-à-vis* the organization in which they operate.

Designing learning strategies and methods : DESIGNING

Developing appropriate training programmes and events has traditionally been the core of a trainer's expertise. The newer term attached to this work is 'learning design'. This would seem an appropriate change in description as the 'learning' that is required may not lend itself at all to the usual 'training' situation, i.e., classroom or course. Further, as newer approaches to developing people tend towards individuals learning for themselves, often from direct experience, the more didactic and formalized teaching skills of the trainer's past become less generally appropriate.

The skills being developed to help individuals learn more effectively away from the job on courses have been described elsewhere. But for most trainers the biggest step in becoming more interventionist will be moving out of the haven of the training school, college or classroom into the organization itself, through more direct contact with managers and staff. To begin this step the trainer needs to be able to design effective 'out-there' activities as integral parts of his overall design.

Some of these contacts can be initiated *as a result* of well-designed training courses or sessions: e.g.

Action planning and implementing

It has been suggested that action planning should be an important element of 'the course'. Trainers will also plan for a variety of action follow-up tutorial visits and the ways they conduct them are important (see 'Follow-up skills' page 110), but they can plan review–clinics back at work; they can set up paired contacts so that members motivate and monitor each other; and there are also a variety of methods available for involving 'bosses' and others *in* action plans and reviewing them to help ensure they get implemented.

Project design

Helping to design projects to supplement formal training is an area of skill with a high premium for the trainer. It will partly depend on how well they know what goes on in the organization. For the project needs to be feasible in practical terms and useful in results terms; and at the same time it needs to be challenging enough to reinforce and develop more formal learning.

Trainers are learning to put much more of their own effort and skill into helping their organization (through managers) identify needs and make use of any training that goes on through project work. Thus they will consider time spent *in* departments, particularly with the managers of their 'trainees', well spent and will plan for this in their design. Results will depend on how well they use this time and this is illustrated later in the section on Enabling (page 110).

Involving managers in evaluating project work also affords the trainer an important opportunity to intervene and helps ensure that training makes a more effective contribution.

Action learning and task groups

This leads to the next step where the majority of the training or learning goes on in the organization and on the job and not in a training environment at all. This can be achieved through 'real' project work where the trainer uses the resources of an action-learning group or set to help learning to happen.

There is a lot of skill involved both in organizing these 'sets' and in helping them work well. The perennial problem is that the 'content' of the projects will be concentrated upon, to the detriment of the 'learning' potential being realized. This, however, has been well-documented elsewhere.

Role clarification

The person's role in the organization is a strong determinant of whether he can apply any skill or learning. Therefore no trainer would leave proper consideration of role out of his learning design if he is at all interested or concerned with more than the individual's acquisition of skill.

Any kind of follow-up activity within the organization offers the opportunity for the trainer to help managers and staff identify possible areas of role confusion and become aware of the consequences. This develops the chance for an important intervention opportunity because it can identify a new area of training need upon which most of the more usual 'training' design depends for its success.

Skill in designing methods to help managers and their staff clarify and negotiate role is essential for trainers who are seeking to intervene and contribute more usefully and effectively in their organizations.

Family groups

Many trainers work largely with 'stranger' groups. A growing tendency, as trainers become more interventionist, is to design learning with and through the actual working group. The design skills are similar to the last section but the trainer has to be very much more aware of the tensions and problems latent in the work group and the serious consequences of the group work exacerbating the problems rather than achieving learning.

Trainers who have not experienced the methods they employ themselves in their *own* working groups may well be taking unprofessional risks with their clients, simply by being totally unaware of the tensions which can arise and get out of control. Work with 'family' and work-groups can take trainers into a risk-area for which many of them may be unprepared or incapable of handling. This is an important area for skill-development.

In all of these methods the trainer's learning design skills are firstly about setting up the appropriate 'structures' to get into the organization, e.g. inviting managers to come to visit courses is a very low-profile, and often ineffective, intervention. On the other hand, building managers' direct involvement through briefing and de-briefing sessions into the whole programme design and establishing it as a prime qualification for course attendance is potentially more powerful. It consequently involves the trainer in higher risk.

Designing the actual sessions with the managers then often needs a skill at least as crucial as designing the formal training course. This will be especially so if the trainer meets the managers in groups on their home ground, rather than inviting them to the training room. Direct contact with managers and staff is an important part of intervening directly and therefore skill in designing such meetings and sessions to meet clear objectives, some of which will be learning objectives, is an essential requirement for trainers developing this kind of role for themselves.

Developing and Organizing Training Resources : RESOURCING

It has often been an important aspect of the 'training function' to develop its own resources. Thus many trainers will be well skilled in the training of instructors and other direct trainers. If not skilled in developing instructors themselves they will regard it as a key part of their jobs to organize effective instructor training through appropriate bodies.

If the instructors and other direct trainers are under the executive control of the training manager and operate in the 'training school' then there should be few problems about their roles and how they carry out their tasks effectively. Problems arise where the instructors and trainers are not a part of the training function, and particularly if they are part-time instructors within departments and have other duties to perform. Role confusion is then a probable source of ineffectiveness; conflicting priorities between instructing tasks and other tasks can present very real problems.

This is where the trainer will need to apply skills which intervene across the boundary between 'training' and the producing or using departments, e.g.:

Clarifying roles of part-time and on-the-job instructors

Trainers need to be able both to negotiate and clarify the roles of instructors with their immediate supervisors and managers and to help them continue to do this effectively themselves. They need to be able to help them set up procedures for using their instructing skills effectively and to design whatever systems are necessary to keep accurate records and monitor progress.

Designing and implementing systems for departmental on-the-job training

Further than this the trainer needs the skills and influence to set up within operating departments the roles and procedures to ensure that the required on-the-job training is carried out and monitored, e.g. there may be a need for a 'training liaison' person in the operating department, simply because the trainer cannot be in all departments sufficiently to ensure that the instructing skills which have been provided are applied and used effectively.

These skills are about developing a 'training capability' within departments that are complementary to the traditional instructor training skills. They are an essential requirement if the trainer is to establish on-the-job instructing; and by their very nature of changing the way departments train and utilize their staff they are intervention skills.

Developing managers and supervisors as trainers

Many trainers use line managers on their formal courses as a sensible and necessary part of 'involving bosses', and thus influencing the use and application of training. Line managers have often benefitted from trainers helping them acquire lecturing and presentation skills, but all this, as useful as it is in practice in improving relationships and building bridges between training and the organization, is merely enabling line managers to act as direct-trainers in a training situation.

At least as important is the skill of the trainer in helping line managers and supervisors carry out their 'training and development roles' *while* they manage and *through* their managing – and this both in their formal roles as developers through appraisal, coaching and counselling sessions, as well as in their informal roles and their day-to-day managing.

If the trainers can be successful in this area they will be influencing directly how the organization is managed and thus more directly intervening in contributing towards its effectiveness. Some of these skills in developing training resources can be provided through formal training sessions – but many of them will be more effectively applied within the organization in the trainer's contacts with managers on-the-job. This is developed further in the section 'Ensuring application of learning' page 110.

Bringing about the acquisition of learning :
IMPLEMENTING

It has been emphasized earlier that this part of the process, acquisition, has only been separated from application because it is currently normal training practice. Trainer skills here are largely concerned with implementing effectively what has been designed' and planned earlier (in the section on designing above). The major shift for many trainers will be moving from more formal, didactic, fully-planned sessions towards more participative, informal sessions which are more flexibly run to respond to the immediate needs of members. This is not to say that well-presented formal lectures have no place in the design and therefore that the trainer's presentation skills are no longer important. But, in addition trainers will have to be aware of the need to develop more learner-centred skills, i.e. they will need to be:

MORE	Guiding	*THAN*	Leading
MORE	Listening	*THAN*	Telling
MORE	Receiving	*THAN*	Pushing
MORE	Responding	*THAN*	Directing
MORE	Observing students	*THAN*	Reading notes
MORE	Aware of all that is going on in the Learners	*THAN*	Concentrating on his/her own 'Teaching'

and consequently *The Learner* will be:

MORE	Active	*THAN*	Passive
MORE	Totally involved	*THAN*	Partly (mentally) involved
MORE	Self-motivated	*THAN*	Being driven
MORE	Self-generated	*THAN*	Being pushed
MORE	Discovering	*THAN*	Being shown
MORE	In control	*THAN*	Being controlled
MORE	Responsible for his/her own learning	*THAN*	Being 'Taught'

It will also be apparent that the *Method* used by the trainer will be one where:

MORE	Time is shared	*THAN*	Taken up by one or few

MORE	Activity is shared	*THAN*	Concentrated on one or *few*
MORE	Members are involved actively	*THAN*	Only *one* or *few* being *actively involved*
MORE	Motivation, interest and enthusiasm may be shown	*THAN*	Acquiescence, lack of interest and boredom
MORE	Depth preparation has been done	*THAN*	May be evident

As with all learning methods, 'small group' work needs to be consciously and deliberately selected and designed to meet the particular learning objectives and training needs which have been determined.

For some trainers, shifting these balances may well be a normal part of their development; for others they can involve a major change in both attitude and role-image.

Ensuring application of learning : ENABLING

If trainers draw a tight boundary around 'learning' which does not include the day-to-day jobs of 'trainees', and if they focus their own activities within the boundary, i.e. the training course or session, then once the trainees have left the training situation the trainers will not have much direct influence on the application of what has been learned. They thus limit their intervention potential and probably the total effectiveness of their training effort in organizational terms. To be fair, it is sometimes the organization itself which draws the boundary and confines training and the trainer within a 'learning acquisition' role.

If, on the other hand, trainers can begin to break through their boundaries in an acceptable way they open for themselves a wide range of intervention possibilities and opportunities for enabling learning to be more effective as it is applied in practice to organizational problems and performance. The newer skills trainers may have to acquire include:

Follow-up skills

Hopefully action plans will have been agreed in the course. Trainers' skill both in enabling plans to be implemented and in helping people learn from carrying out their planning will often be a more significant determinant of how much relevant learning goes on than their 'traditional' teaching skills in the formal course.

Not only will coaching, counselling and group-participation skills be crucial in this area of work but ability and willingness to understand a variety of work problems and situations will largely determine the trainer's effectiveness. In addition, skills in defining problems in different ways and ability to *apply* problem solving skills will also contribute towards effectiveness in follow-up sessions.

Above all trainers are now in a position to 'teach by example' outside their own territory; and their ability and willingness really to listen and to observe will be on test.

They may well have to cope with, and on occasions confront, resistance and hostility from more senior managers, so ability to influence without any executive authority to back them will be an important part of their armoury.

Project tutoring

Many formal training courses now have 'project-work' as a part of their overall design. At worst this is just tacked-on to the course as a rather academic exercise often 'done for the tutors' and assessed by them. At best projects can be a basic, well-integrated element in the whole design and an essential factor in the application and extension of learning.

It is imperative, and almost goes without saying, that the project must be of real practical use to the individual *and* his organization. Further, 'bosses' and those that influence performance need to be involved in developing and evaluating the project. Thus trainers will rarely keep project-tutoring to themselves; they will rather involve as many key staff around their 'course members' as is feasible. In this way trainers will have opportunities both to influence direct application of their learning design and to develop useful contacts for further development of learning opportunities.

Role negotiation

In many follow-up and project contacts the trainer will have noticed that roles within the organization are often confused. This leads to ineffectiveness and waste and is very often the basis of much of the friction and poor personal relationships within the organization. Trainers need to be particularly skilled in negotiating and clarifying their own role *vis-à-vis* the line manager and 'trainees'. Thus, acting as an example they can help managers ask and face up to the appropriate questions about their own roles.

Involvement in clarifying roles is particularly a very powerful intervention activity for the trainer; it could be argued that it is an imperative pre-curser to any 'skills' training. Lack of clarity of roles could be a major reason why much of the trainers' effort in helping staff aquire skills has not resulted in effective application, and consequently in benefits to the organization.

On-the-job learning

Acquisition and application have only been separated in this sequence because that is the common practice of most trainers at present. Thus trainers currently need to develop their off-the-job training course activities to initiate opportunities inside the departments of the organization, but there is an increasing trend for trainers to be able, and to be allowed, to operate directly within the organization. Their skills in helping people learn *directly* from experience then become increasingly important. These have been covered earlier as they are similar to follow-up skill and include listening, coaching and counselling, group leading and participating skills. But the ability to help group decision-processes and learning-processes, which many trainers will have developed in their own training sessions, becomes particularly important as 'family-teams' grapple with real-life problems.

In these activities the trainer will be applying skills more related to an Organization Development Consultant than to traditional teaching-skills.

Gaining support for action : CATALYSING

It is clear that when trainers are operating directly inside departments they are afforded the opportunity to influence other things which may be barriers to people either applying useful learning or bringing about change.

Helping to clarify roles is only one aspect of this work. If this is done effectively it invariably provides data for line management which will help them design more appropriate structures. It is significant that many organizations will invest considerable sums in improving people's ability without giving any attention to the appropriateness or effectiveness of the organizational machinery within which the abilities must be applied. Trainers who also give no attention to this within their organization are, it could be argued, colluding in the mis-use of training investment.

Obviously to get involved in influencing the organizational structure and the systems and procedures which help it work demands far more of trainers than merely 'teaching people skills'. There is far more risk involved – and this is possibly the key skill that trainers who get involved in catalysing organizational 'support' action have to develop; coping with the increased risk-taking. All the other skills identified in the last section become important here as the trainer develops the capacity to act as a 'learning consultant' within the organization in addition to acting as a trainer within the training department or function.

This is one area where expertise from outside the immediate organization unit has advantages. Not only is there the possibility of greater objectivity, but a wide experience from outside the actual unit can help provide the line managers with the different perspectives they may directly need.

This is probably one of the reasons why internal trainers are not often invited to play this wider role in their organizations. Their skills in achieving the required influence in other ways may then be crucial in helping the organization both to learn what it needs to learn and in gaining proper benefit from its existing training effort. Some of these other ways may be the trainer's relationship with and the use of, or assistance by, outside agencies.

Checking organizational results : EVALUATING

Much of training evaluation and assessment in the past has been backward looking. Most of the key publications deal with assessing the training effort in its own terms and only a very small proportion of what is written deals with ultimate measures in business terms.

The current Training Intervention Process looks two ways inward into the Learning Design and Application and outward into the identifying of need and the application and support of what has been learned. Earlier Evaluation Research has resulted in the development of a two-way or figure-of-eight evaluation cycle. Accepting that a large proportion of training activities are currently divorced from direct contact with the organization a two-way evaluation activity is required which leads to two kinds of evaluation/assessment skills and techniques to be developed by trainers. For example see Figure 5:2.

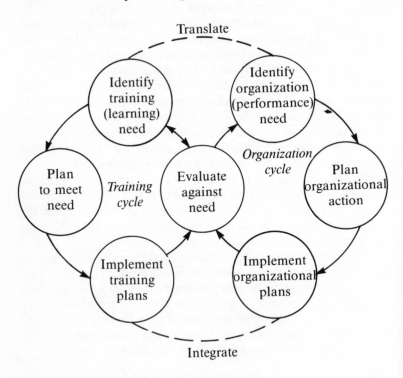

Figure 5.2   Two-way evaluation cycle

This model is not ideal as it accepts the separation of Training and Training Needs from the organization and, therefore, from what are more complex organization needs, the resolution of which requires more than training can achieve in isolation. (This again emphasizes the key 'linking' skill which the trainer can contribute to translating organization needs and problems accurately and appropriately into learning needs.)

However, it does identify an important area of skill required by trainers, i.e. that of evaluating training activity in organizational terms. In this it is essential that they involve both 'trainees' and the managers who identified the needs originally. It is in their currency that the results must be measured. The trainer can then help them collect the necessary data through a variety of methods.

Clearly trainers will need a good understanding of the various methods of data collecting and interpretation and have expertise in questionnaire design and sampling techniques, but equally important is their ability to provide the structures and the motivation for line management to measure what has really been *their* investment in a training activity in their own terms.

What is fairly certain is that if the trainer achieves this state of affairs then the evaluation in organizational currency is more likely to lead managers to becoming aware of other learning needs and to motivate them to pursue them rather than convincing them that nothing more needs to be done. The harsh spotlight of this two-way evaluation will help trainers and their organizations pinpoint weaknesses in the whole process. This is possibly why both trainers and organizations tend to avoid it.

CONCLUSIONS

Finally, focusing on the centre of the cycle, the key skill for all trainers is the ability to exploit and develop the opportunities they are offered. For it is as they make effective interventions into the way the organization works that they will be able to demonstrate the contribution training can make. As they continue to do this in the wider and more vital processes of the organization, their roles will develop an increasingly interventionist character, and they will become more effective in helping their organizations change.

ASSESSING YOUR INTERVENTION POTENTIAL

Training is only just beginning to develop a strategical dimension. Projects and programmes have usually been developed on an *ad hoc* empirical basis – and this at certain stages of development is appropriate. But there comes a time when the empirical data needs a framework for designing a total strategy, and this is the basis of the cycle of skills we have just described. It can be used to check that any current or proposed training effort includes all the necessary activities and can help to ensure that the whole intervention strategy is successful in bringing about change.

For example, the 'cycle' can be used to help trainers assess their intervention potential. Although it is in no way a precise tool it can give a useful indication of self-development needs if trainers are willing to be constructively self-critical. Try these three exercises:

Exercise 1. Awareness of time and effort spent in a current training programme/project.

Consciously shift your effort and time spent by estimating, logging active time and planning your next pattern of activities.

CATEGORY	Estimated time spent on activities in the category	Actual (logged) time spent	Planned time for next project
DIAGNOSING	= %	= % ⟶	%
TRANSLATING	= %	= % ⟶	%
DESIGNING	= %	= % ⟶	%
RESOURCING	= %	= % ⟶	%
IMPLEMENTING	= %	= % ⟶	%
ENABLING	= %	= % ⟶	%
CATALYSING	= %	= % ⟶	%
EVALUATING	= %	= % ⟶	%

Exercise 2. Identifying personal development needs.

Under *each* category answer as objectively as possible:

1   What skills am I currently applying effectively:

2   What skills have I available which I am not applying:

3   What skills do I need to develop in order to improve effectiveness in this category.

Check your own assessment with that of a professional colleague and draw up a plan of 'intervention' skill development and application.

Category	Skills to develop
Diagnosing	
Translating	
Designing	
Resourcing	
Implementing	
Enabling	
Catalysing	
Evaluating	

Exercise 3. Planning future intervention strategies.

Take as an example an important training initiative you are starting to plan. In the light of the last two exercises decide now the kinds of activities you will include in each category which in the past might have been missing. (This might merely mean a shift of emphasis and time on to *Translating* or *Enabling* or *Evaluating* activites compared with *Designing* and *Implementing.)* Determine a plan now to achieve a good balance in activities around the whole cycle.

Intervention category	New activities planned
Diagnosing	
Translating	
Designing	
Resourcing	
Implementing	
Enabling	
Catalysing	
Evaluating	

The cycle of interventions is not intended as a straight jacket which will 'plan the life out of' your training effort. It simply offers a set of signposts which will help ensure that your interventions:

are more appropriately balanced
are linked together coherently
and take training *into* the organization.

In this way they will have a better chance of directly and effectively influencing your organization's ability to change.

FURTHER READING

This chapter has drawn upon the author's earlier work, partly funded by the Manpower Services Commission. Other published sources of this work include:

Jones, J.A.G., 'Figure of Eight Evaluation – A Fundamental Change in the Trainers Approach', *Training Officer,* Sept., 1981.
Jones, J.A.G., 'Making Trainer Interventions more Effective', *Journal of European Industrial Training,* 1982 vol. 6, no. 6.
Jones, J.A.G., 'Training Interventions Strategies – An Opportunity to Develop the Role of the Manager', *Training and Development* Sept., 1983.

On other related aspects, the following sources will be found helpful:

Argyris, C., *Intervention Theory and Method,* Addison-Wesley, Reading, Massachusetts, 1970.
French, W.L. and Bell, C.H. (Jnr), *Organizational Development* Prentice-Hall, Eaglewood Cliffs, New Jersey, 1973.

These are both 'classics' that have had a considerable impact on our thinking and practice regarding change, organizational development and the use of 'intervention' strategies.

Hurst, W.C., 'Coping with Change – Use the Action Learning Approaches',*Industrial Training Services Ltd., Monograph,1981.*

6 The Modern Management Developer

Charles Margerison

Over the last twenty years management training has been one of the main growth industries. With it has come a new profession called management trainers, developers and educators.

We are professional advisers, but we come from many different professional backgrounds. Indeed, management training must be the most multi-disciplined and multi-skilled profession that there is. However, it is noticeable that very few of those people who practice as management educators, trainers and developers have any formal training in what I believe to be the central core of our profession – in educational processes and principles.

Although anyone who is seeking to educate or develop people at the primary and secondary level is required to have formal educational training, this requirement is waived when it comes to the tertiary and post-experience levels. This has always surprised me. If it is vital for people who are educating and facilitating the learning of people under the age of 16, why is it not essential for those who are doing the same for those others who are over the age of 16?

Most management trainers, educators and developers have therefore learnt 'by the seat of their pants'. It reflects the very youth of our profession. The rewards that are available to those who are competent are extremely high, reflecting the way in which the demand for such service currently far outstrips the supply.

Therefore the first recommendation I would make to improve our training effectiveness is that we first attend to our own professional development. It is indeed a question of 'Physician, heal thyself'. One of the great creeds of modern management training is self-development. I believe there is a need for this to be organized in a concerted way rather than just left to individual motivation. To this end we need to look at the qualifications that we should require of management educators and developers.

The other area we need to put a lot of energy into is understanding in depth the needs of our clients rather than just giving them what we think is best. The more we can involve them the more likely it is we will be effective and regarded by our clients as professional. It is therefore with this key issue that we start.

WHAT DO MANAGERS WANT US TO DO?

We should start by looking at what our clients are asking us to do. By taking a market orientated approach we can identify the needs before we 'rush in where angels fear to tread'. The consulting aspect of our work is a prime requirement in which we should become effective. If we do not know what people want then it is very difficult for us to adapt our knowledge and skills to the requirements.

Once we have established what people are requiring of us then we should have a framework within which we can begin to design and develop appropriate interventions. To this end we need to have good understanding of our contribution within the context of the educational theories that have been put forward. We can then start to meet the requirements through consultative research.

About ten years ago I became interested in why some managers were promoted to high positions and others were not. I initiated a study of the careers of chief executives. Initially this was done in the United Kingdom with over 250 chief executives participating and then in the United States with over 700 executives. Therefore within the context of the Western industrial culture the results should be of interest to us as trainers, particularly as there was a high degree of consensus independent of the country or the size of organizations involved.

The research shows that executives who have been successful attribute the prime reasons for their success to themselves, not to us as trainers. Indeed our professional contribution comes very low down on their list of factors which they believe influence them. For example, special off-the-job management training was rated eighteenth and nineteenth in the list by the UK and USA managers, respectively. Indeed a sound technical training rated higher at fourteenth on the list of factors and this in itself is indicative. The factors which managers on both sides of the Atlantic rated highly were:

1 a need to achieve results;
2 an ability to work easily with a wide variety of people;
3 a challenge;
4 a willingness to take risks;
5 early overall responsibility for important tasks;
6 a width of experience in many functions prior to the age of 35;
7 a desire to seek new opportunities;
8 leadership experience early in their career;
9 an ability to develop more ideas than colleagues, and
10 being stretched by the immediate bosses.

The message seems to be that we as management trainers need to look more carefully at the personal and situational factors which surround managerial development and achievement. Senior managers identify themselves as people who wish to direct their own learning within the context of a challenging work environment.

One argument therefore is that we should spend more time to structure on-the-job learning situations rather than designing off-the-job management courses. Perhaps we would be more effective in identifying the high achievement orientated individuals and structuring their career opportunities so that they can learn from doing. This would certainly be in line with the principles and proposals advocated by Professor Reg Revans who has long argued for structured development through action learning.

This puts the emphasis more on our facilitating rather than on our training skills. We need to be far better at our consultative work in understanding the needs of managers and then helping create the environment and situation within which they can learn and get feedback on their performance.

WHERE DO OUR CLIENTS NEED OUR SUPPORT?

More recent work has led more into exploring what work managers need to do in order to be effective. There was an opportunity to investigate the key aspects of their work in some detail. A particular interest was their need to improve their skills in managing others and an understanding of their own and others' strengths. The focus was on how they managed their team of people and gained the skills to do it better.

The areas which we identified as critical to their success in team management are as follows:

Innovating — the identification of ideas and innovations which can improve the way the work is done.

Promoting — the persuasion of others and exploration of how people and resources can be acquired to the task.

Developing — the development and assessment of practical methods for doing a task.

Organizing — the organization and implementation of particular systems and matters to get a task underway.

Producing — the regular production and output of the task to a set plan and standard.

Inspecting — the detailed inspection and monitoring of the task to establish standards and regulations.

Maintaining — maintenance of the cultural and physical resources to ensure the task is done in accordance with values, principles and beliefs.

Advising — the generation and presentation of information relevant to the task.

Linking — the ability to co-ordinate and integrate various aspects of a team's work in order to get the work done.

All these are integral to what we have called Team Management. Therefore in our work we need to find out within the above areas where managers want us to put our efforts. Should we help them become more innovative or concentrate on how to strengthen their skills in inspection or organization? Of course most managers if asked will say they wish to be strong in all areas. However, research using the Team Management Index as a measure shows that managers have distinct preferences and strengths in at least three or four of the above areas which need to be updated and other areas where they need to learn how to develop their strengths or delegate more.

We have therefore developed a set of maps which managers can use to begin to identify where the needs are. The Team Management Wheel shown in Figure 6:1 is one example of how we can begin to assess what their training needs and requirements are.

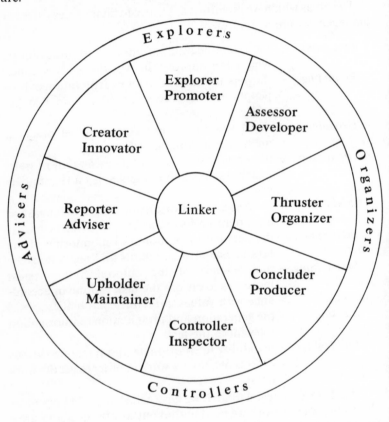

Figure 6:1   The team management wheel

We have been able to provide personal feedback through descriptive 3000 word profiles based on the results from the Team Management Index. It has been well tested for validity and reliability. It is now used in a number of industries such as oil, banking, manufacturing and airlines. It is possible to identify managers' work preferences and feed these back as a basis for discussing their training needs within the context of their jobs. This approach provides the technology we need in order to engage in proactive facilitation. Managers are looking for us to go beyond process consultation to give them some tangible means for identifying their requirements for which they can then take personal responsibility.

THE EDUCATIONAL ARCHITECT ROLE

Increasingly we have to combine the skills of the consultant with that of the educator in what can be called educational architecture. Just like an architect we need to discuss with our clients what needs they have and then bring our design skills to bear on the issue. In this we therefore need to be skilled in consultancy and have a good educational base on which to develop our contributions whether they be classroom-based or action-learning centred.

Generally, we as trainers need to understand the trends that are occurring within the managerial world which are going to have an impact on our own profession. These demand that we take more of an 'existential' view of management development. By this is meant that we should look more carefully at the existence of our managerial clients and seek to design interventions which support them and help them confront the realities that they face. While managers are concerned about team management and the tasks that they have to do, it is within the context of their own existence and development. The more therefore we can understand the existential reality of our clients and their careers the more likely it is that we will be able to contribute. Our work on managerial work preferences using the Team Management Index and Wheel as a method of mapping is one example of how this can be done. The move toward existential management development will involve a number of key factors which we need to understand and manage. These include the following:

From teaching to resourcing

We will spend far less time in the classroom and be required to work alongside managers more in the field supplying the resources 'in an on-line basis'.

From programmes to contracts

We will have fewer formal management education programmes and instead move to short-term learning task contracts. Here managers will be working with us to fulfil a task rather than absorb static knowledge.

From individual to group orientation

Instead of training individuals we shall move towards more of a team-work orientation. In short we shall be expected to work with teams of people rather than just deal with a collection of individuals.

From standard to real cases

Managers will be less interested in cases which do not relate to their job and organization and we therefore will need to become far more proactive in providing real cases based on their organization from which they can learn and develop.

From delegating to developing

We shall see managers taking far more responsibility for the development of their own staff and asking trainers to support this. This will be a change from delegating such responsibilities to trainers.

From top down appraisal to bottom up appraisal

The appraisal process is a key to any management development. In the future we will be asked to work with managers to identify their needs based upon self-appraisal. This will therefore again drive the training function more into a consultative supportive role.

From product centred to market centred orientation

Instead of putting forward a series of training products we will be expected to design interventions whether they be workshops or action-learning activities to meet the needs of what our client managers want. This will mean that we shall have to be far more flexible and adjust to the needs of the market.

From teaching inputs to business outputs

Alongside the above changes we will therefore be measured less on the input we make (training sessions run) but more on output in terms of the results achieved and the context of the actual business and the effect our work has on management performance.

From fixed to continuing education

We shall also be expected to be involved directly in the move towards the continuing education of all managers. No longer will the short, fast, quick injection of a course be sufficient. We will be expected to plan with managers for their continuing development throughout their career and have on-going discussions with them as to how they can develop their understanding and skills in a practical and active way.

FROM STATIC TRAINING TO ACTIVE EDUCATIONAL ARCHITECTS

These therefore are the changes and developments that we see occurring. They are already in progress. Many of us have already moved in the direction of becoming educational architects. The measures by which we shall be assessed will therefore change. It is likely that the demand for our services be the major measure. In short, the link between management development and organization development is moving even closer. We shall not be seen to be relevant as trainers unless we can have an affect upon managerial and organizational performance. Clearly we are not going to succeed with managers unless we understand their world and reality and unless they feel that we have got something to contribute. To this end, therefore we need people who are going to develop proactive skills not so much as communicators of the word but facilitators of the word. In order to achieve this, trainers have got to get out from behind their desks and out of the classroom and also away from the day to day routine of administration to work with managers and their teams. Our work increasingly is in the field and at the 'coal face'. When we use classrooms it should be to relate with real work issues. We must move more and more to be at the centre of the work task and involve ourselves in the existential reality of the jobs of those people we seek to serve.

CONSULTANCY SKILLS

As a profession we need to become far more demanding of the training that we impose upon ourselves and others who intend to work in the field.

No management educator and developer can do an effective job unless they are able to work with their clients, to understand their needs as a basis for designing an effective process of improvement. Consultancy skills, therefore, are crucial. We need to develop a training programme which can be assessed and evaluated in normal ways, which enables members of our profession to not only acquire the knowledge that has been developed associated with consulting skills, but the process skills as well. I have made an effort to do this within my own courses as an integral part of our MBA programme. The students react very favourably to the programme because they say it enables them to practice and develop skills in the essential process of working with clients to try and improve performance. This means, in practice, understanding the theories of organization development and change which must, in my view, underlie any improvement/ change process whether it be at the individual, group or total organizational level.

A lot of people may say that the consulting process is not subject to systematic training. However, there are specific skills in the various stages of consulting with clients which have been well researched. In my own work I have identified the following as key areas in which we can build our skills:

1   Identification
2   Diagnosis
3   Contracting
4   Data management

5   Feedback
6   Implementation and follow-through.

Let us examine each of these.

Identification

So often we are given cues and clues which do not either recognize or pick up the gap. A person may talk to us obliquely about a particular issue and unless we are aware and able to handle the dialogue, we may not get to the heart of the matter. This is the equivalent to the initial discussion that the doctor may have with the patient. We, like the doctor, have to be quick at picking up the cues and clues offered and understanding the implications of these. We need to know what to look for and how to respond. This kind of sensitivity can be developed by specialized training in looking at particular cases and practising 'conversational control skills' to encourage our clients to share with us their concerns, doubts and fears. Indeed the whole skill of relationship building is critical to our success as management educators.

Diagnosis

The second step in the skills we need to develop, therefore, relate to thinking through and diagnosing the needs. This may be an identification of the problem. However clients may actually have done their own diagnosis. In such situations they may want more a diagnosis of options and ideas in terms of a basic design for tackling the problem. Much of my own work involves sitting down with clients and discussing the issues they face and seeking to work out an overall plan of campaign in which they would have some confidence.

Contracting

This then leads us into another important area – that of contracting. Just as a builder can talk to you about the construction of a new house and identify the needs, there comes a point when a contract has to be drawn. This will involve an assessment of costs and a more detailed outline of what needs to be done. In our field of management education it is not always easy to be specific about the particular stages and costs in advance. However, I do believe that we could become more effective in the way in which we contract with our clients. I know from personal experience that my own management development initiative would have been far more effective if I was better at contracting and establishing who does what, when, how, and where, much more clearly in advance of the activity to be performed. Therefore contracting and contract-negotiation are key skills.

Data management

The next stage usually involves gathering data and is more closely aligned to research skills. There are a number of courses taught on research methods in various disciplines. Management educators and developers need to be aware of these, ranging from the personal interview through to the formal questionnaire, and be aware of the strengths and pitfalls of formal sampling methods as compared to the informal sensing methods. Generally this is one of the key areas of weakness that we, as a profession, have. There is a tendency to use a rather limited range of data gathering approaches, and sometimes to over-formalize the arrangements. For example, people often rush in to use repertory grid, simply because that is a technique which they have acquired, whether or not it is relevant to the situation at hand.

Indeed, in many cases it is best to gather the key clients together for group discussions rather than to use highly sophisticated methods. This, however, is no reason for us to ignore the range of methods available. It is important for us to be well trained in their use and to know when and how to use them.

Once we have collected the data, we need to be skilled in data analysis. This again is part and parcel of any sound research methods course. It involves everything from being able to understand the use of computers in the analysis of data through to being aware of the ways and means of coding qualitative data. Several authors have gone on to provide a range of analytical procedures and we all need to be trained in their use more effectively than we are.

Feedback

Having gathered data and analysed it, we come to the critical stage of feeding it back. It is here that there are probably as many mistakes by management education and development professionals as in any other area. So often we have done a good job on the content side but fail to communicate back to the clients in a meaningful way. In any formal training that we were to establish to improve our profession, hard and detailed practice on feedback would be well spent.

In particular, this can be linked with the ability to handle criticism. Very often executives, when they get feedback, want to attack the data and those who present it, in some form or other. This is often seen as a personal attack on the individual who is giving information. Therefore in the data discussion phase it is vital that we learn how to manage the interaction with our client, whether it be at individual or group level. There are personal examples where senior executives have set out to test me at a personal level by challenging the feedback in a most aggressive way. It is here that I have drawn on process-consultation skills and tried to work on the feelings expressed rather than defend, apologize or attack the individual concerned.

Implementation and follow-through

It is here that we need to develop our understanding of how to work with clients in order to seek improvements. Management development covers such a wide area of activity ranging from individual instruction through to helping groups redesign the way they work together. Therefore there is no golden formula for implementation. Again it requires rigorous training which enables people to gather the experience from a wide number of interventions. This can only come from on-the-job applications. However, these can be facilitated by training as an integral part of our improved professionalization to ensure the transfer of training back to the work place before we rush off to the next assignment.

These steps are common to most of our assignments. They are understood as the circular process which we continually have to go through in order to understand what is required to put forward some proposals often as a result of joint consultation and then be able to follow them through. All of these stages are subject to training and all people who are moving into the profession of management development should become more skilled at each level. We need to start training ourselves before we train others.

EDUCATIONAL THEORIES

In order to do the above we also need to have a very sound theoretical base upon which to build our activities. While we will not always end up in a teaching role we will, nevertheless, always be involved in helping people to learn and develop in order to improve their performance. It is therefore essential that we really do have a thorough grasp of educational theories and research.

In the way in which we carry out our job as management development professionals, we have various approaches which invariably have some root in a theory or principle. Over the years a considerable body of knowledge has been developed on various educational theories and their applicability.

One way in which we might develop our professional expertise would be to incorporate into our own personal development a more thorough understanding of these theories as, for example, outlined by Bigge (1982). It would not necessarily, however, immediately improve our practical performance. For example, there are many singers who do not really understand the rudiments of musical theory. However, it would provide a basis upon which we could consider our options and know how to comprehend the practical application within some body of principle.

There are a number of theories which need to be considered in the context of management education and development. Some are more important than others. The ones listed here (Figure 6:2) are the most interesting.

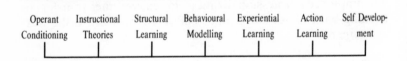

| Operant Conditioning | Instructional Theories | Structural Learning | Behavioural Modelling | Experiential Learning | Action Learning | Self Development |

Figure 6:2   The learning spectrum

Operant conditioning

This approach, strongly put forward by B.F. Skinner (1979), builds upon the original stimulus-response research conducted by Pavlov. In essence what Skinner has proposed is that rather than just reacting to a stimulus we can be conditioned to respond in various ways. This is a most important principle, not only of learning theory but also of management. Indeed, many line managers actually do implement Skinnerian theory in the way in which they structure the organization and set out the various reward systems.

Likewise we, as management developers and trainers, should be more aware of the principles and practices associated with operant conditioning. The words such as 'conditioning and reinforcement' are now part of our vocabulary. However, the number of controlled experiments on operant conditioning in the management education arena is relatively few. Some of the principles have clearly been applied in the work that has been done on improving people's memory and also in the area of the work of stimulating creativity.

More recently a number of management developers and educators have used the principles of operant conditioning in trying to help managers cope with stress and strain. Furthermore, although the principles are not normally referred to explicitly, a number of the courses dealing with motivation and reward systems have as their background the principles associated with operant conditioning.Therefore, although the original research of Skinner, which was done on animals, may seem to be far removed from the world of managerial work, it is important to consider its applications. Probably the most important area of all in the light of modern technological development and change is that associated with computers and the way in which managers and staff can control their own environments or alternatively be controlled through the use of machinery.

Instructional theories

In their basic form instructional theories have been with us from the early days associated with talk and chalk. The lecture is still probably the most over-used training approach, even though we know it has limited value in improving a person's skill.

Today we need to question whether we should start with practice or start with theory and work to practice. It is interesting if one takes someone on to a golf course and starts to instruct them in the game. Do you first tell them all of the rules and then talk to them about the various clubs before actually asking the person to strike a ball? Alternatively, do you take them to the practice ground and ask them to hit a ball before telling them anything about the game? Theories of instruction therefore are central to our whole profession and need to guide our educational practice. In most cases we tend to start in management education and development with the lecture and work to practice, assuming we are talking to people with some experience. We probably over-stress the instructional side and do not work enough on drawing out the experience of those who are involved in the process of learning.

Structural theories

It is here that Jerome Bruner (1960, 1966) has made an important contribution, initially from his research on the development of young children. He emphasized the need for people to have an understanding of the structure within which they were learning and also to have a willingness and readiness to learn. Too often we recognize as management developers and educators that we are working with people who have been sent on courses. Therefore we are dealing with people who are going through the motions.

Bruner's contribution has been to widen our focus and understanding of the conditions under which people learn. Therefore it is important to work out a strategy even before people come along to a formal learning experience as to what their prework involvement should be. To what extent should they be consulted on the learning? To what extent should they be prebriefed? To what extent should they be asked to do pre-coursework? To what extent should they be on a course at all? All these are questions on the structure of learning. In this we are looking not only at the pitch on which people will learn but the perceptions and purpose that they have and bring to the process.

Far more attention therefore needs to be put on the environment surrounding the learning process, otherwise we shall be concentrating on only a limited area. Probably the more important area is the place in which people will actually practise their learning and we need to understand more of this in order that we might structure the learning so that it is relevant to their needs. It is this that Bruner and his colleagues have stressed, that we must build in a structural context which relates to the requirements of the learner. Managers themselves must have a firm input on this.

Behavioural modelling

The ideas of behavioural modelling have been long discussed. At their simplest level it is clear that we can learn by observing and mimicking other people. In terms of learning theory, Albert Bandura (1977) has taken these principles and studied them in some depth. In the process he produced a theory of social learning which we in the field of management development and education need to examine. At its most practical it is no doubt true that a manager who acts as a mentor is in fact acting as a social learning model. Whether the actual manager appreciates and knows this and understands the principles from which he is working may be a moot point. However, as management educators and developers it is important that we guide and advise on best practice.

Clearly simple, down to earth modelling is not sufficient. Each person must not only watch and observe and copy and learn from others but relate that to their own personal style of operating. It is here that we should be able to advise and guide and counsel.

This is particularly so when one introduces video feedback. This is a particularly powerful medium for being able to learn by observing oneself as a model in comparison to others. This is one particular area where we, as management development and training professionals, can begin to use the principles of social modelling to improve managerial performance.

Experiential theories

Much of our work in management education and development is done through simulations. We set up role plays, we create exercises, we run case studies and a host of other methods to enable people to practise. This clearly is a most useful method as it can reduce, both in terms of time and cost, the expense involved in helping people learn.

Considerable work over the years has gone on to look at the effect of experiential learning. Probably the most wide ranging studies, particularly in the areas of role play and case examples, have been carried out by Norman Maier (1963, 1982). His work shows clearly that group decision making, problem solving, interpersonal skills and other areas associated with the management of people can be improved in terms of skill developments through the use of experiential methods.

The work of Pfeiffer and Jones (1972) and their handbooks

have provided a rich array of methods for us to use. Of all the methods in use, I believe the experiential methods are those which have been most favoured by management educators and developers. However, little attempt has been made to assess the impact of these methods in the way that Maier did. We need far more effort put into understanding not only the theoretical base of experiential learning but the testing of those theories to see whether or not our methods, however creatively designed, actually work in practice. This involves us in the transfer of learning and follow-up.

Action learning and self development

More attention is being focused on real job learning rather than classroom based activity. Professor Reg Revans (1982) has led the way with his clear call for a learning-by-doing focus within a well organized system. He has referred to the need for 'comrades in adversity' to share and compare their experience and ideas. In this way argues Revans we can begin not only to solve real problems but learn at the same time.

This sounds straightforward and even obvious. But it demands of ourselves, the training specialist, particular skills in organizing the arrangements as Revans has shown with his work in hospitals, banks, and manufacturing organizations. It requires special skills also in being a 'set adviser' or consultant to those in the action learning programme.

All of this has been recognized by the International Management Centre from Buckingham which has established the first Master of Business Administration programme based exclusively on action learning principles. No one can take part in this learning programme unless they have a project, are supported by their organization and immediate boss, pass the stringent entry tests and also pay the tuition fees. The programme has successfully taken off in not only the UK but Malaya, Singapore, Hong Kong, Kenya, South Africa and other places. It is a move towards existential management education. However this form of learning is not only task based: it is linked closely to an individual's self-development. Each person has an image of who they are and what they can be. Increasingly people are taking charge of their own learning and seeking the resources to achieve the goals they set. This is an integral part of existential learning and we as training professionals need to learn how to resource such diversified needs.

SUMMARY

We as a profession are both old and young. Teachers have been a cornerstone of modern civilization. However the industrial organization based trainer is a relatively new role. We are still searching for our role at the managerial level.

It has been proposed that we need to develop as educational architects and work with our clients in a market orientated way. This will require a move towards an understanding of the existential realities of the managers we serve. We will need to concentrate more on the process side of the relationships rather than just the content side. This will mean a closer involvement with the politics and a more proactive role in identifying the key issues in a consultative relationship. The world of training demands a multi-skilled approach, building on educational theory to meet the demands of individuals accountable for getting work done through teams against time and cost criteria. It is a challenging assignment requiring skills of the highest order. We should therefore look to our own self-development as a continuing prime objective if we are to be effective working to advise and support others.

THE HONEST MANAGEMENT DEVELOPER'S CHECKLIST

1   Have I received sufficient training for the job?
2   Do I know what my clients really expect of me and of the training events I run?
3   Do my training events contribute in a real sense to the development of managerial effectiveness?
4   Do I draw upon the available knowledge of what makes for managerial effectiveness?
5   Do I spend enough time in structuring on-the-job learning?
6   Do I place enough emphasis on team development?
7   Have I the necessary skills and qualities to be an effective development consultant?
8   Do I understand enough about educational and learning theories to be able to use them effectively?
9   Do I know what key self-development goals I should be pursuing in the next two years?

If your answer to any or all of these questions is 'no', then you should seriously be looking at either a different job or at ways of enhancing your skill and experience. A systematic programme of self-development will be called for.

If your answer to most or all of these questions is 'yes', then you clearly know what you are about and should get on with it. But please don't neglect your own, continuing self-development.

REFERENCES/FURTHER READING

Some of the material in this chapter has drawn upon a variety of sources – including the author's considerable international research. You may wish to read further in some of the areas covered. To help direct your further reading, we have grouped the sources in categories that relate to particular aspects of management development covered in the chapter.

Learning theories and approaches

Bandura, A., *Social Learning Theory*, Prentice-Hall, Englewood Cliffs, New Jersey, 1977.

Bigge, M.L., *Learning Theories for Teachers*, Harper & Row, New York, 1982.

Bruner, J.S., *The Process of Education*, Harvard University Press, Harvard, 1960.

Bruner, J.S., *Toward a Theory of Instruction*, Belknap, 1966.

Maier, N.F.R., *Problem Solving Discussions and Conferences*, McGraw-Hill, 1963.

Maier, N.F.R., and Verser, G., *Psychology in Industrial Organizations*, Houghton Mifflin, Boston, Mass., 1982.

Margerison, C.J., 'Existential Management Development' in C. Cox and J. Beck, (eds), *Advances in Management Education*, Wiley, 1984.

Margerison, C.J., 'Where is Management Education Going?' in A. Kakabadse, and S. Mukhi (eds.), *The Future of Management Education*, Gower, 1984.

Mumford, A., 'The Role of the Boss in Helping Subordinates Learn' in G. Taylor, and G. Lippitt (eds.), *Management Development and Training Handbook*, McGraw-Hill, 1983 (among Mumford's other well-known work on learning to learn and learning styles).

Pffeifer, J.W. and Jones, J., *Handbook of Structured Experiences for Human Relations Training*, University Associates, San Diego, CA, 1972 onwards

Revans, R., *The Origins and Growth of Action Learning*, Chartwell Bratt, 1982.

Skinner, B.F., *Beyond Freedom and Dignity*, Pelican Books, 1979.

Wills, G.S.C., *Demonstrable Productivity from Management Education*, MCB University Press, Bradford, 1984.

Managerial and team performance

Margerison, C.J., 'How Chief Executives Succeed', *Journal of European Industrial Training*, vol. 4, no. 5, 1980.
Margerison, C.J., and Kakabadse, A., *How American Chief Executives Succeed*, American Management Association, 1984.
Margerison, C.J. and McCann, D.J., *How To Lead a Winning Team*, MCB University Press, Bradford, 1984.
Margerison, C.J., and McCann, D.J., *The Margerison McCann Team Management Index*, MCB University Press, Bradford, 1984.

Consultancy skills

See Chapters 3 and 5 of this book, and also
Lippitt, G., *Organizational Renewal*, Prentice-Hall, Engelwood Cliffs, New Jersey, 1982 Chapter 12.

7 Policy Power

Howard Silverfarb

Developing a training policy for an organization is frequently viewed as the dreariest and least attractive task of the training professional. As such, it is often the one given the least attention and the minimum amount of thought and detail.

This is unfortunate. No truly successful training effort can be either produced or managed without a sound philosophical base, and a well planned, carefully implemented and vigorously administered policy.

The development of an effective training policy need not be a drudgery at all. In fact, it can and should be a creative and purposeful document from which the entire direction and framework of the organisation's training springs. Without it, the training has no meaning or goal; with it, the path is well set out and clearly understood.

This chapter will deal with what a training policy is and why have one, what it can do and what it should encompass. In addition, we will touch on who should formulate and administer the policy, how it is arrived at, and its actual preparation and establishment. Also included will be sample introductory policy statements, full training policy documents, and responsibilities and resources allocation statements. The chapter will conclude with how to obtain approval and support of the training policy, as well as actually communicating and administering it.

WHAT IS A TRAINING POLICY?

The preparation of a training policy is one of the first steps to be taken when setting up a training function. The policy:

is the basic statement giving the function its license and character. It defines its scope and responsibility. It has roots in the basic policy of the overall organization. It shows clearly just how training is expected to contribute to the achievement of the goals of the organization (Craig, 1976).

WHY HAVE A TRAINING POLICY?

There are three main reasons for having a training policy:

1   it 'clarifies the company's position (on training) without the need to create a complete set of rules and regulations to try to meet every possible situation' (Skills Development Fund, 1985);
2   it provides a set of guidelines setting out how training and line staff can carry out their day-to-day training responsibilities, and
3   it 'establishes a framework within which more detailed (training) plans can be developed' (Singer, 1977).

THE IMPORTANCE OF A TRAINING POLICY

A policy is essential to the planning and implementation of a training function, since without it 'each piece of training will be carried out in isolation without regard to the overall needs of the organization' (Singer, 1977). Thus a policy creates a sure goal direction for all who participate in or are affected by the training.

WHAT DOES A TRAINING POLICY DO?

An agreed policy 'will identify the scope of training in the organization'(Lastra and Nichols, 1978). In addition, 'once programs are planned with regard to policy, it is much easier to prepare a budget to justify expenditures'. At the very least, the training centre and the organization 'will agree on what (the) training operation is all about'. However, a training policy statement 'does not describe exactly what should happen in a given situation – apart from saying that something should, providing that there is a need'.

WHY PUT A TRAINING POLICY IN WRITING?

Whenever possible, the policy should be in writing. That may not be welcome in some organizations, since they 'hate to obligate themselves in a general way'. Nevertheless, a written policy commits the training function to its own and the organization's objectives. It gives the department much needed visibility, and can serve to motivate and enthuse training staff.

The danger, of course, is that training and the organization do not live up to the policy, either day-to-day or on a longer-term, conceptual basis. This is the risk that the professional takes in order to create a top-quality, highly-regarded training effort.

WHAT SHOULD A TRAINING POLICY INCLUDE?

A training policy should, at a minimum, include a general statement of:

first, what are the ultimate ends of training in (the) particular organizational setting, and, second, what are the fundamental principles underlying training and how can these be utilized, given the constraints of (the) organizational environment (Otto and Glaser, 1970).

Indeed, a policy must answer the question: 'How will training contribute to the goals of the organization'?

More specifically, the policy should indicate 'resources the company will devote to systematizing training and the provision of training areas and materials'. It should also include reference to 'who gives and receives training, what courses and programs will be offered, when training will be conducted, how it will be conducted, why it should be given in the first place, and where it will be given'.

Should training professionals desire, and should they feel that the organization would accept and support the principles, they may wish to state the following in the body of the policy:

1   Introductory and skills training, related to actual job requirements, must be mounted for all newly-hired and transferred employees prior to their assuming their positions.
2   The training will be made available only to staff who are deemed to require it for either the job they are presently doing or one they will be doing in the near future.
3   The company is committed to the 'total development' of all staff members (or, at the very least, selected 'high potential' individuals) in accordance with their interests, their capabilities and the organization's needs.
4   The training will be practical, job-related and skill-oriented, and will use the most modern and efficient training methods to achieve its objectives.
5   The training function will choose the necessary instructors, i.e. among its own staff, line management or outside consultants, to ensure the best quality training to meet that particular need, given reasonable budgetary constraints.
6   The training nomination procedure, both for in-house and outside courses, can be initiated by either employees or their manager, with further approval required of the training department and perhaps the personnel or administration division.

WHO SHOULD FORMULATE AND ADMINISTER A TRAINING POLICY?

The job of co-ordinating the development of the policy lies with the training director or, as sometimes referred to, the 'skills development co-ordinator'. He should not simply be a receiver of policies worked out by higher-level management, but must play a key role and be included in (even insisting that he be included in) its original formulation. The actual policy, however, is finally set by top management.

HOW IS A TRAINING POLICY ARRIVED AT?

Training policies, and skills development policies in general, are arrived at in much the same way as other company policy. The way in which they are cascaded down the level follows a sequence similar to these other policies. This sequence can be represented graphically as shown in Figure 7:1.

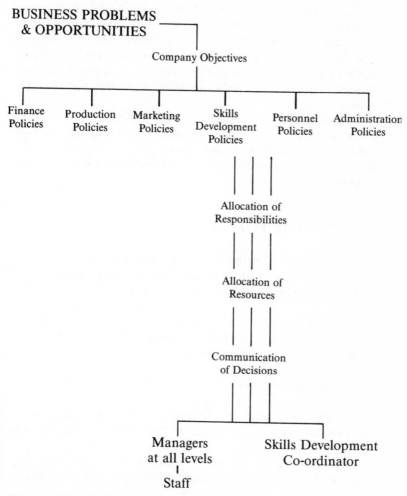

Figure 7.1   Policy development

BEFORE MAKING THE POLICY

Before the policy is drawn up, the training director learns of the company's near and long-term goals and puts together a framework within which the policy will be formulated. This framework will include a list of possible policy areas which, if introduced, could help to meet the training needs that the organization's objectives would suggest.

The training director would then check with higher-level management to determine what are their expectations of the training effort and whether the policy framework is in keeping with the company's objectives. The 'framework' can be used here as a working paper from which the training professional can direct focused and detailed policy-making decisions with his top management.

Following those discussions, the training director can outline a tentative training policy. He may then begin to gauge, through contacts with managers throughout the organization, their potential support and their future participation in carrying out the proposed policy.

MAKING THE POLICY

A training policy, as with all other policies, is expected to endure. As much time as is possible should go into developing it. It should be revised periodically and reviewed at least once every two years.

Its text should be in the form of statements written so that they are flexible enough to handle related situations but specific enough to avoid misunderstanding.

The introductory and general policy statements

The policy introduction should indicate what a training policy is and why have one, its importance to the training effort, what it is meant to do and who prepares and administers it.

A general policy statement describes the reasons for the establishment of a training function and the position the company takes on training and development.

The content of the introductory statement has been covered earlier in the chapter. The general policy statement may begin by simply justifying training itself, as follows:

Training is *not* a 'cost' factor in business but rather an *investment*, the results of which, both savings and actual profits, are the 'dividends'.

In an effective training effort, the firm's *investment* in training facilities, personnel and training time should be more than made up for by the management and officer time and effort saved, and the productivity gained, as a result of the structured skills learning.

And greater *profits* are realized both as a consequence of this extra time and the increased productivity of a more efficiently and more quickly trained employee.

The statement should go further and tie training into the organization's goals. It should also state management's commitment to training, the role of managers and the training director, and how specific training approaches will be developed. An example is shown in the box overleaf.

1 Training, like any other plant activity, is expected to help achieve the goals of the organization. Training has no value unless it helps eliminate deficiencies and achieve the organization's goals

2 Training should never be regarded merely as an 'activity' but rather as a management tool for changing individual behaviour and improving plant efficiency.

3 The effectiveness of a plant's training effort depends upon the extent to which management is committed to support it; the proper assignment of responsibility to line managers and training specialists; and the skill with which the training is planned, implemented and evaluated.

4 Both line managers and the training director have important roles in and responsibilities for the training effort. Each manager must accept the development of his or her people as a prime responsibility, include it in objectives and be willing to be appraised on the basis of how well the goals have been achieved.

In addition to stating the basic training philosophy, we find it necessary to develop specific training approaches related to the particular plant involved. The training director must develop these on the basis of information gathered when the training situation is assessed. Each addresses the particular problems unique to the environment in which the training department will operate (Lastra and Nichols, 1978).

The body

The text in the main body of the policy should detail the ultimate goals and anticipated results of the training. In addtion, it should state who will give and receive the training, what programmes will be offered, and when, where and how they will be conducted. The 'how' refers to the various methods to be used in the training.

The body of the policy may be relatively long and quite elaborate. Or, in keeping with the organization's needs and desires, it may be quite short and perhaps less detailed.

Two examples of abbreviated training policies and two examples of more elaborate training policies follow.

A medium-sized company

'The company recognizes that training and the development of skills are fundamental to its continued efficient and profitable running; it is not to be regarded as an amenity but as a primary factor of prosperity, which is essential to the development of the company's most important and expensive asset – its employees.

The Company Training Officer will assist the management in the preparation and running of training programmes, but the responsibility for training lies with all members of the management and supervisory teams in their respective departments.

The company will further implement this policy by granting day-release to members of staff who are able to benefit from a recognized and approved day-release course. Release from work without loss of remuneration will also be granted to members of the company who attend approved courses, either residential or local' (Singer, 1977).

A rapidly growing local bank

'The large number of new recruits is of concern to management. In a competitive domestic banking market, (we) are especially concerned with the need to offer and maintain a high standard of service to customers. The training policy of the bank therefore focuses on entry level training, especially for counter staff, to equip them with the job skills, and knowledge of the organization, its services and goals.

The company realizes that its public image of efficient

and courteous service can be enhanced or marred by its frontline staff. The company therefore considers it of prime importance that all counter staff go through a planned programme to induct them into the organization. All new employees must attend the company's induction course. This is to be immediately followed by job training. In this way, no new recruit will be allowed to attend to customers before completing, to an acceptable standard, the training programme' (Skills Development Fund, 1985).

A small public-limited service company

'A systematic and purposeful approach

We believe in learning and training that is systematic and purposeful. Our approach to management development is carefully targeted and organised to help upgrade participants' knowledge, skills and attitudes. This leads to better organization and management in support of our company's larger corporate objectives and goals. Our approach should be regarded as part of a long-term, continuous and complex process by which our managers and supervisors improve their ability to perform, and gain the rewards of enhanced job satisfaction.

A comprehensive and integrated approach

We believe in learning and training that is comprehensive and integrated. Our approach is comprehensive in its scope by covering not only the commonly regarded essential elements like planning, organizing, directing and controlling, but also knowledge, skills and attitudes in areas of topical concern and likely future need such as stress management, self-awareness and social responsibility. Moreover, it is an integrated approach rather than piecemeal, in which each component relates to the previous and succeeding elements in the programme, employing one "common language". An integrated approach to management development, of course, implies the need for an effective corporate infrastructure in terms of manpower and succession planning, management by objectives, performance appraisal, career planning and development, and corporate planning.

An experiential and practical approach

We believe in learning and training that is experiential and practical. We emphasise a highly participative approach encouraging "learning by doing", since skills cannot be learned by reading about them or listening to a lecture. We also, however, recognise the need for balance – balance between theory and practice. Theory is necessary to the extent that managers and supervisors must know and understand why they are encouraged and trained to behave the way they are as well as what makes themselves and the organisation effective. Practice without understanding is pedestrian and mundane at best, understanding without practice is inevitably ineffectual. So we subscribe to the principle that there is nothing so practical as good theory – good theory in terms of effective management and supervision, training practice, and what works well for our organisation.

A tailor-made and job-related approach

We believe learning and training should be tailor-made and job-related. While many trainers employ training packages and packaged approaches, we recommend training methods and content that are tailored and relevant to our organisation and the participants themselves. We often draw up material that is obtained "from the horse's mouth", i.e. by prior discussions with selected likely participants, our own training staff, managers and top management. We employ our managers, as much as is possible, as training resources, whether in the preparation and presentation of on-the-job or formal classroom courses, in those areas in which they are best able to offer and transfer their skills. In any case, we ensure realism, job relevance and credibility in the eyes of the participants. We believe this facilitates both useful conceptualisation and practicable skill development.

A caring and professional approach

We believe learning and training should be caring and professional. We insist on the very highest standards of knowledge, skill and commitment in our professional work. We endeavour to remain at the leading edge of development in the training field and to display the state of the art in terms of creative ideas, useful research and best practice. Our professional approach entails the establishment and maintenance of good rapport through the fine-tuning of our style and methods in order to provide the best possible learning environment.

An evaluated and cost-effective approach

We believe learning and training should be evaluated and followed up to check its success. We aim to maximise the cost-effectiveness of our programmes and feedback to our management its measurement. We do this by evaluating participants' opinions about their training experience, by evaluating changes – improvements – in knowledge, skills and attitudes, by following up participants later to evaluate application and ensure changes in behaviour on the job, and by evaluating on-the-job and organisational performance improvements. We report both quantitatively and qualitatively to management, together with recommendations for any necessary or helpful further action.

An enjoyable approach

We believe learning and training should be enjoyed. Pleasure undoubtedly enhances the learning environment. We encourage social events, lunches, dinners, and get-togethers as part and parcel of this wherever possible – and we are noted for our sense of humour!' (Gill, 1985).

A multinational bank's regional training centre

'General goals and objectives of the bank's regional training

1. For all participating staff

a. To upgrade and improve, where necessary, the banking knowledge and skills of all existing officers and clerical employees, to include their introduction to new computer and banking-related techniques and procedures;

b. To implement a programme of job rotational training and development, in order to create a pool of experienced and motivated officer and clerical bankers capable of filling the bank's immediate and long-range transfer, departmental back-up and staff promotion needs.

2. For participating clerical staff

a. To educate newly-inducted clerical employees in banking and the structure and role of the bank, as well as to thoroughly prepare them in a specific skill so that they may immediately and productively perform their assigned banking function following the training.

b. To train selected officer-candidate personnel in supervisory and banking skills, including the techniques of managing people, time and work.

3. For participating officers and manager staff

a. To upgrade and improve, where necessary, the banking knowledge and managerial skills (decision-making, delegation, organising, controlling, etc) of existing lower and middle-level regional officers and managers.

b. To prepare selected individuals in this category for further advancement through higher-level technical banking management training and education.

c. To educate newly-inducted university graduates (management trainees) to banking in general, and the bank's policies and procedures in particular, in order that they may be prepared to immediately assume officer responsibilities following their training.

d. To train selected regional and world-wide bank employees, as well as individual client staff, and government programme and institutional personnel, in various introductory orientative or full-scale technical banking or management skills learning.

e. To solicit both the participation, as well as to prepare officer and management staff, in the techniques of on-the-job and formal classroom training, in order to create a bank-wide, ongoing commitment to the regional training effort.

4. For the Regional training staff

a. Through the introduction of "training-the-trainer" programmes: to teach training centre personnel and branch training correspondents how to train staff effectively.

b. To develop and implement a carefully structured programme designed to localise the regional training function.

5. Miscellaneous goals and objectives

a. As a result of the training and employee development programmes, to motivate employees to a greater sense of belongingness and identification with the bank, its ideals and aspirations.

b. To create a "central clearing house" of region-wide banking studies information, school and outside consultant organisations,. which are or can be made available for specialist bank and management training and secondment.

c. To develop an in-house library of banking and banking-related publications and study materials.

d. To help in the preparation of, and provide the facilities for, top management conferences and seminars; to plan and co-ordinate marketing and information forums for corres-pondent banks and investment clients; and to arrange useful training-related functions for those organisations and banking customers of particular interest and importance to the bank.

6. Anticipated results of the regional training

It is intended that after a minimum of 3 years, the following major programmes will have been initiated:

a. All new clerical and officer (management trainee) personnel entering the bank will have received a formal induction programme, followed by an intensive job skills training, before being assigned to a specific banking function.

b. All candidates for promotion and transfer, whether at the officer or clerical level, shall first receive a skills training befitting that function (including management skills training) before commencing their new assignment.

c. A planned, systematic programme of employee develop-ment and rotational training will have been started.

d. A co-ordinated, region-wide exchange programme will have been formalised between the various bank branches, in order that new and existing regional officer and manage-ment personnel may have the opportunity to visit, train with and share each other's individual and branch-wide knowledge and expertise.

e. A resource centre of banking and training knowledge and information, including outside course availabilities, will be open to all the participating regional personnel.

f. A deliberate "training effort" involvement of managers and supervisors (at all levels) in the preparation, presentation and follow-up of both formal and on-the-job training, will have been started.

g. A realistic set of target dates will have been formulated, (and the plan already well-along toward realisation), for the localisation of the regional training effort.

Who shall do the training?

A. Training as a total effort

For the regional training effort to be an effective and ongoing part of the bank's structure, it is imperative that it be considered a "team effort", involving not only the training staff itself, but all the bank's officers and managers.

1 *The bank supervisor as a trainer.* This is because training is a continuous responsibility of supervisory personnel, and can never and should never be totally "delegated" to a separate training function.

Thus, it must be clear that the effort *will not* replace the supervisor's own involvement, but will instead help him to enhance his training effectiveness.

The training will obviously make use of the supervisor's long and varied experience in his individual specialities, aid him in communicating his skills both formally (in the classroom) and on-the-job, and fill in the many gaps that may result from his lack of both training expertise and the time that he can devote to the effort.

2 *The regional training staff as trainers.* The regional training staff itself shall be made up of personnel located at the regional training centre as well as one full or part-time correspondent located individually in the major participating branches.

The preparation of training materials and their presentation, and the training follow-up, are primarily the responsibility of the training centre staff, with the work of the correspondents more heavily emphasizing the latter two over the first. These duties refer both to formal and on-the-job training, and take into account not only the training staff's own personal involvement but also that of the bank officer staff whom the trainers will be expected both to initiate into the effort and to help improve their training expertise.

B. Outside banks, institutions, schools and training consultants

In addition to training developed by the regional staff, it may become necessary and desirable to employ outside bank educators and training specialists for various bank-related programmes. Lack of time, unavailability of in-house expertise, impracticability, cost factors, various training facility needs and certain other constraints might require such utilisation.

How shall the training occur?

After the training needs and priorities are identified, a series of steps leading to the actual training and its follow-up occur.

If non-existent, a job description of the job to be trained for is prepared, followed by a step-by-step breakdown of each task required in that job (detailed task analysis).

In the meantime, the individual(s) needing the training (those who will be required to utilise it on-the-job immediately afterwards) are identified, and their present job knowledge is determined. The difference between those present abilities and what is actually necessary for the job is the 'gap' which the training must fill.

During the process, a determination is also made as to what is the appropriate form for the training: formal (classroom) or on-the-job; in-house instruction; or training at an outside bank, school, institution or consultant organisation.

If the training is in-house, a determination also must be made of who will provide the training: the officers, certain management personnel, the training staff itself or any combination thereof. Shall the training be mounted in the training centre or at the branches, and when and for how long shall it continue?

Finally, the actual training materials, including the audio-visual aids are prepared, and the course, whether management or clerical, commences. The training method-ology which has proven to be the most effective, the 'Socratic' or 'discovery' method, is employed, and the trainees are encouraged in participatory learning and practical application through numerous banking-related case studies, role plays, 'hands-on' and 'Model Branch' simulations.

The last and probably most important stage in the training process, ensuring on-the-job application of the skills after the instruction, is begun immediately after the training ends. The success in transferring the learning into actual job performance must be the goal of any training, and as such it is the sole measure of its effectiveness. Included in this stage is 'follow-up' and 'review', which can modify as well as determine future course content and teaching methodology.

Where shall the training occur?

In addition to the regional training centre, the training of personnel may also be mounted in the branches or at local or overseas venues.

A. At the regional branches (formal and on-the-job training)

In regard to many of the formal and on-the-job training programmes developed in the regional centre, it will often be expedient to have them taught in the individual branches with either the involvement of a correspondent or one or more of the regional training centre staff. When such a need arises, a suitable room or work area can be used temporarily for the instruction.

B. Outside training (local and overseas)

This mode of training will not be confined solely to the region, but rather the decision to use outside programmes will be based on a determination of whether they offer the best available known instruction in that particular speciality taking into account, of course, reasonable constraints of time and budget' (Silverfarb, 1977).

INCORPORATING A RESPONSIBILITIES STATEMENT INTO YOUR TRAINING POLICY

Occasionally, training directors develop separate statements for training responsibilities and resources allocation, rather than have them included as part of the formal training policy. This is done both to emphasize their importance and to lessen the chance that their approval would be jeopardized should the policy itself be questioned or delayed.

The purpose of the responsibility statement is to spell out who is responsible for the skills development functions. It lists out what supervisory officers must do. It also gives the training manager a central co-ordinating role.

A sample responsibilities statement might read as follows:

All supervisory officers are to identify such individuals reporting to them, chart their career paths and provide the necessary grooming in the form of job rotation, management/supervisory development, and personal skills in presentation, communication and human relations where a need is identified.

The Training Manager is responsible for identifying common skills requirements in consultation with department heads and, where cost-effective, should plan for in-house programmes rather than draw on a variety of external resources for each individual.

INCORPORATING A RESOURCES ALLOCATION STATEMENT INTO YOUR TRAINING POLICY

The objective of a resources allocation statement is to ensure that everyone concerned is clear about the exact nature of resources to be allocated for skills development.

The following is an example of such a statement:

External resources such as management schools, management consultants and course providers are to be tapped when necessary. Programmes conducted outside office hours are to be preferred. However, release on full pay for up to four months may be granted to outstanding employees.

Apart from common skills requirements under the charge of the Training Manager, areas of need specific to the company are to be met by structured in-house programmes. These are to be conducted on company time, although their schedule is to be the least disruptive to work.

The Training Manager, in liaison with supervisors, is to put up the development plan and budget for the CEO's approval. This should include expenditure on necessary equipment and materials.

APPROVAL AND SUPPORT FOR YOUR TRAINING POLICY

Prior to finally announcing the policy to the organization, it is essential that the training director check with and get the needed approval and support for the document from higher-level management. If the director did his job right, and provided continuous feedback to essential management every step of the way, this should be nothing more than a simple formality. If he hasn't, and the policy gets delayed or derailed, he has little choice other than to go 'back to the drawing board' or attempt to 'sell' the policy in the same or a modified form. The latter course is a dangerous one, since a training policy should be 'top management driven'. Unless the training director can influence or change corporate policy, he has little chance of convincing top management to alter their policy to fit his.

The director should also check the final document with the company managers, especially those whose support and later participation he needs to ensure the effort's success.

COMMUNICATING YOUR TRAINING POLICY

The policy is now ready to be communicated to the entire staff. Since it's fairly certain that at one time or another the policy will have an effect upon everyone in the company, the 'need to know' is indeed company-wide.

This policy dissemination can be done by notice, circular or newsletter, or by whatever means is usual to that organization. In addition, managers should hold meetings to explain the policy in detail.

ADMINISTERING YOUR POLICY

No policy can prove effective unless it is carefully administered and followed-up. The training director must regularly determine whether it is being adhered to. This can be done informally, especially when the organization is small, by his or his staff's observations and from standard manager reports and interviews.

Since the training department is expected to take the initiative in carrying out many of the provisions of the policy, it will often be expected to perform a self-policing function. Larger organizations may require strict and more elaborate controls, perhaps including the formation of a management or training advisory committee. The committee, or the training department itself, must review the policy at regular intervals to determine whether to add to, modify or change its provisions.

CONCLUSION

A systematic and effective training function begins with a well thought-out policy, tied to the company's strategy.

As Zenger (1985) points out, training functions that get close to the heart of the organization are usually very effective. Your policy must reflect your organization's policy. In conclusion, we present a checklist that will help you get your policy 'right'.

A CHECKLIST FOR FORMULATING, COMMUNICATING AND ADMINISTERING A TRAINING POLICY

Before you make the policy

1   Did you learn what are the near and long-term goals and objectives of your company?

2   Did you put together a framework within which to formulate your policy?

3   Did you speak with higher-level management to determine what are their expectations of the training effort?
    - their views on training responsibilities?
    - their views on resources allocation?

4   Did you outline a tentative policy based on these views and expectations, as well as your own experience?

5   Did you gauge the potential support and future participation of the managers in carrying out this proposed policy?

Making the policy

1   Did you put the policy in writing?

2   Did you write the policy in the form of statements?

3   Is your policy flexible enough to handle related circumstances, but specific enough to avoid misinterpretation?

4   Did you start with an introduction to the policy?
    - what is a training policy?
    - why have a training policy?
    - its importance?
    - what is it meant to do?
    - who prepares it and administers it? why?

5   Did you include a general policy statement?
    - the reasons for establishing the training function?
    - what position the company takes on training and development?

6   Did you include in the body of the policy:
    - what are the ultimate goals/anticipated results of training in the organization?

- who give and receives training?
- what course programme(s) will be offered?
- when will the training be conducted?
- how will it be conducted (methodology)?
- where will it be conducted?

7 Did you include who will be responsible for training actions ('responsibilities statement')?

8 Did you include the exact nature of the resources to be allocated for the training ('resources allocation statement')?

9 Did you check with/get the approval/support of higher-level management for the policy?

10 Did you check with and get the support and promise of participation from the managers?

Communicating and administering the policy

1 Did you effectively communicate, by notice, circular or newsletter, the agreed upon policy to all staff?

2 Did you hold (a) meeting(s) to explain the policy in detail?

3 Do you check from time to time to determine whether the policy is being adhered to?

4 Do you review the policy at regular intervals to decide whether to add to, modify or change its provisions?

REFERENCES/FURTHER READING

The following sources have been drawn upon in the preparation of this chapter. Some are specifically concerned with training policy and philosophy – the others are more broadly based but include sections on training policy.

Policy specific

Gill, R.W.T., 'Our Training Philosophy', *Roger Gill and Associates' Mission Statement,* 1985, pp. 2–4.

Lastra, B., and Nichols, M.B., 'Define and Broadcast Your Training Philosophy', *Training,* November 1978, p. 387.

Silverfarb, H.I., 'Training Policy', *Multinational Bank's Regional Training Centre Principles and Practices,* 1977, pp. 2–10.

Skills Development Fund, Republic of Singapore, 'Getting the Framework Right', *Notes for Managers Series 2,* 1985, p.1.

Broadly based

Craig, R.L. (ed), *Training and Development Handbook* (2nd ed)., McGraw-Hill, 1976, pp.2–6.

Otto, C.P. and Glaser, R.O., *The Management of Training,* Addison-Wesley, Reading, Mass., 1970, p.10.

Singer, E.J., *Training in Industry and Commerce,* Institute of Personnel Management, London 1977, p.33.

8 The Trainer as Manager

Peter Bowen

In this chapter we consider an approach to the management of corporate training based on the requirements of high-performance business organizations and of the people we can expect to find in such organizations. Implicit in the approach described here is the idea of 'balance' or 'contract' between organizations and their memberships. This is helpful in any review of the contribution of training to the performance of an organization.

Indeed, in any such review we need to make this contribution explicit. Too often what happens in the name of training is less than specific. This blurring of identity is unfortunate, and costly. It suggests an imprecision which undervalues training as an instrument of management control. It also suggests that a good deal of what is sometimes undertaken in the name of training is insufficiently targeted and inordinately expensive.

The effective management of a training function should begin with an explicit statement of purpose, and a clearly defined contribution to the organization in which it is located. It should continue with the design and delivery of a performance-related method of training which is geared, first, to the measurement of skill performance and, second, to the improvement of performance where weaknesses are acknowledged to exist. It should end with a recognition by the organization that the competencies whose performances have been reviewed in training are valid. This enables the training sequence to begin again, but at a higher level of effectiveness than before.

Training functions are best considered in this way, as cycles of activity geared more or less purposefully to the organizations in which they exist. We can develop our understanding of what promotes effectiveness in the management of training by an examination of the following propositions:

1   Strategies for business should incorporate strategies for human resource development.
2   Human resource strategies are about the performance of skills.
3   The purpose of training is to develop the capability of people to perform skills to defined standards of competence.
4   Standards of competence can be improved, and it is a purpose of training to advance standards of performance.
5   Gearing planned improvements in the performance of human skills to planned improvements in the performance of the organization links the strategy for human resources to the strategic plan of the organization.

This is the primary cycle of training activity, and its successful accomplishment is the main criterion of effectiveness of the training function.

INTEGRATING HUMAN AND BUSINESS STRATEGIES

There are two aspects to this topic. The first is about how to create a human resource strategy within a wider corporate plan. The second is about the corporate infrastrucure of training required to maintain the vitality of the training cycle. Let us consider each aspect in turn.

Building the human resource strategy

The first requirement of an effective training function is that its purposes derive from the objectives of the organization as a whole. Whether training is organized centrally or more diffusely, the risk is that training is permitted to go its own way. The result is usually disastrous for both the organization and its training function.

Conversely, successful organizations are identified increasingly by the existence of a human resources strategy. Typically this will be a strategy in which the training and development programme occupies a central position. Successful organizations build in training to their operations as a way of life. Sometimes this conceals the energy which organizations need to invest in the strategic development of the human resource programme if the business is to advance effectively.

In principle, the importance of correctly positioning human resource strategies within wider business planning frameworks is acknowledged by corporate planners. In practice, the quality of 'fit' between planning for the business and planning for people is less than satisfactory. Individual human resource plans for pay, careers, roles, representation, development, security, benefits, and the rest are drawn up at different points in time. People plans are often formulated during periods of organizational growth, with insufficient flexibility for contraction and slack. Plans for people can erode more rapidly than marketing and financial plans. Above all, the assumptions which inform an organization's human resource planning may be far less explicit than those which govern the construction of its marketing and financial plans. For such reasons planning for people presents inherent but not insuperable difficulties for strategists and planners. Nevertheless, successful organizations can and do accomplish long-range planning for the development of people.

Most organizations have an obvious need to pace performance. Similarly, many will need to establish, review and revise performance futures within some kind of strategic business plan. A human resource strategy geared to busines results will have identified and clustered those policies aimed at the improvement of people importance at its cutting edge.

Building a human resource strategy in this way takes us down two pathways. The first is that we must model the strategy in stages similar to those required in any corporate plan. The second is that we need to construct people policies with a rigour comparable to other corporate plans. Figure 8:1 sets out the main steps of strategic planning, including human resource planning.

1 Assess the future environment
2 Set out the assumptions and guidelines
3 Develop the broad objectives
4 Define the specific targets
5 Construct the plans and budgets
6 Implement, with performance indicators and review

Figure 8:1 The steps of strategic planning

This step sequence illustrates the outlines of a human resource planning cycle. We can place a time-scale on the sequence of, say, one year or more ahead of the present. Whatever the scale, a discipline of making explicit a preferred course of action is imposed, with a methodology of comparing and evaluating actual against planned performance of the preferred action.

In Figure 8:2 are set out some typical elements of a human resource strategy. Some are more concerned with the performance of people. Others are aimed at the improvement of security or at the protection of rights in employment.

1 Organization structure and management style
2 Communication
3 Productivity
4 Remuneration and rewards
5 Benefits and entitlements, including pensions
6 Discipline
7 Career planning
8 Job evaluation
9 Security of employment, including severance and redundancy arrangement
10 Health, safety and welfare
11 Representation
12 Training and development

Figure 8:2 Typical policy elements of the human resource strategy

This list is offered to illustrate the likely human resource policy interests of a large organization: there is no suggestion that organizations actually conform in detail. Within the total range, however, emphasis will be given in 'achieving' organizations to performance-related policies.

The integration of selective people policies for high performance has been approached by Walker (1979). Here a 'building block' method is suggested where relevant policies for staffing an organization are clustered around a core human resource strategy. Figure 8:3 illustrates this process in respect of manning and organization. Note how the cluster of policies depends upon the existence of a human resource strategy, the key building block in the set. But the use of policies in each case varies according to the task.

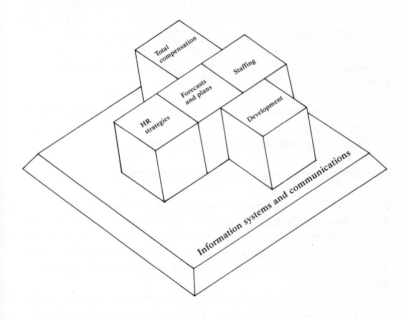

Figure 8:3   People policy building blocks

Based on work by James W Walker (1979).

If, for example, a key objective of the human resource strategy is to secure and retain a higher calibre of manager in the organization, then the use of policy frameworks like those in Figure 8.3 will be relevant. The pursuit of other key objectives will involve different frameworks.

But in organizations whose business performance is required to progress measurably year on year, we repeat that the human resource strategy will need to be similarly performance orientated. This means that the strategy must ensure the development of people in ways which enhance their capabilities. It must also be along lines which maintain a sense of equity and trust between organizations and their memberships. It is in this sense that the planned improvement of human performances must proceed, and why the notion of 'contract' between employers and employees is so important in this respect. The positioning of a training and development policy in any cluster of performance-related policies is critical for this reason: training delivers benefits to both the organization and the membership. The human capability of the organization to achieve its business targets is increased by training, but so is the personal competence of each individual. This is the nature of the contract.

The construction of a performance-related training policy is discussed in more detail in a subsequent section. We turn now to the second aspect of integrating human and business strategies: creating a corporate infrastructure of training.

Creating a corporate training infrastructure

Clustering high-performance human resource policies, including the training policy, to align with the requirements of the business strategy of the organization is a first condition of effective management of the training function. The second is to create the means by which a training policy is implemented across the organization.

Training strategy, and the policy which delivers a strategy, is the property of the organization. Effective training requires the organization to communicate from the centre to the parts the objectives, authority, style and structure of a training policy and the plans and programmes which stem from it. Typically, the mandate to train comes from the directorate at the centre, but the licence to continue comes in reality from the line.

For these reasons an organization should review its training function at more than level. Centrally, there is a need for a strategic review conducted at least annually. Here the directorate needs to confirm the value and vitality of its training investment, and especially in terms of its performance contribution to the business. This strategic review should be complemented by a more frequent scrutiny of training activities at the level of each separate division or individual business unit of the organization. Divisional reviews at something like six monthly intervals are recommended.

At both levels, however, the chairmanship of these reviews should be conducted by the principals of organizations: managing directors for strategic review, divisional or business unit directors for divisional reviews. In this way the ownership of training is reinforced.

It is well worth the time and effort involved in getting this right. Effective training management depends upon a partnership between line management and trainers. Where training is conducted by training specialists for line management, the maintenance of confidence is vital. This requires the active influence of the line in determining and renewing its training plan. The most obvious sign of decay in such partnerships is when senior line management becomes indifferent to its own training.

However, such issues of ownership and involvement in training by the organization are eased considerably where the programming of training can be cycled into time-phases with distinct beginnings and ends. An important condition for effective training is where cycles exist: timeless training is a prescription for boredom and apathy. This involves the creation of a training year into which programmes can be inserted and removed, for which objectives are set and plans prepared, and by which results can be evaluated. As far as possible, training and financial years should be identical. Above all, the development of a training strategy needs to occur within a predictable and measurable time framework.

The method of communicating training to audiences within large organizations is an important part of the corporate infrastructure. It should occur at predictable times within the training year, and provide a regular opportunity to update potential users on availability and content. The need for line managers to be familiar with the details of a training plan for their business unit is critical. The best way to do so is to issue a standardized guide to training year on year. Reinforcing the training message in a consistent format and at regular intervals ensures recognition and response.

At the core of the training infrastructure is the training plan. Here what is determined in advance in the training reviews described above can be keyed into the next cycle as a new training activity. In this way the content and quality of training advances from one cycle to the next. Effective training requires a planned response to need. Each major division of the organization should be encouraged to construct and agree its periodic training plan specifying the objectives, priorities, programmes and content of what is available during the current cycle, and what is likely to change in the next.

PERFORMANCE-RELATED TRAINING

Integrating the business strategy with a human resource strategy geared to the planned improvement of people performance is the first global requirement of an effective training function. Without this perspective, training is likely to remain out of focus. From such a standpoint, however, the pattern of a training strategy for high performance emerges much more clearly, and this we go on to describe.

The requirement for a strategy may well begin with quality issues of management, arising from developments or changes in the strategic business plan. For example, the organization misses new business opportunities because its existing management cadre is too narrowly specialized. Or its career planning indicates an insufficient supply of quality candidates for new positions created by expansion. Or because competition for the organization's business is increasing, and the skills of people are insufficient to match the pace.

These are not unfamiliar situations. The business changes, the human resourcing lags, an opportunity is missed. Always a cost is incurred. The aim of a performance-related training strategy must be to sharpen as well as to broaden the human capability of the organization to adapt to new situations. How can training make a direct contribution to the bottom-line performance of the organization?

Training functions are vulnerable to criticisms of performance blindness, failing to incorporate explicit targets, controls, or indicators of performance. Performance-related training counters such criticisms. Designed at W.H. Smith by the author, and developed with his colleagues, this approach to the training of managers and staff emphasizes how:

1   Effective training depends upon identifying the key skills of jobs and exercising their performance to defined standards of competence.

2   Identifying skills, defining standards and exercising performances requires a distinctive training methodology. This methodology involves the profiling of skills to identify individual strengths and weaknesses, and a personal skill development plan where performance improvements are required.

3   Skill development can be undertaken by residential training, by directed self-study (open learning) or by both methods. It may address procedural deficiencies, practical skill requirements or knowledge-based weaknesses.

4   The purpose of performance-related training is to appraise relative skill performances and to produce the swiftest possible learning response. An effective learning response is accomplished when a performance improvement can be demonstrated in the skill under review. This is achieved by the administration of a final exercise.

Performance-related training became fully operational in W.H. Smith in 1986. During 1985 the methodology of profiling management skills performances was developed to:

- identify lists of core skills;
- ensure the authenticity of these lists;
- identify standards of competence in the performance of each skill, and similarly ensure the authenticity of these standards;
- devise benchmark tests and exercises to allow managers to demonstrate performance in relation to a standard in each skill under review, and to satisfy participants of the fairness of these exercises;
- administer a management skills profile to each participant, and
- devise a personal development schedule to improve skill under-performance to an acceptable standard of competence.

We can make two generalizations about this approach. The first is that a skills or competence based approach to training, one which is the primary characteristic of performance-based training, is the correct approach to the performance development of people in organizations. This is especially true of managers and the development of managerial cadre, and it is with managers that performance-related training should commence.

This emphasis upon skill and competence is vital in the growth of achievement and performance-orientated training strategies. And it is upon the measurable improvement in key skills that the approach advocated here depends. The argument for this is summarized as follows:

1   The source of identity in work is the practice of skilled activities.
2   The ownership of skills provides individuals with personal stimulus, targets, and standards.
3   People seek regular opportunities to improve skill performances, and to receive critical feedback on both stronger and weaker performances. Properly presented, such feedback provides a more powerful and a more enriching environment for individual learning and development than other, less demanding, approaches to training.
4   The most sensitive technique of feedback is that provided by a profile. Here all the relevant skills for, say, a particular level of management in an organization can be profiled together, and a balanced picture of strengths and weaknesses derived.
5   The possession of such a personal profile of achievement against standards is a vital pre-condition of focused development where skill deficiencies can be identified clearly and where skill improvements can be driven by learning, and subsequently re-profiled. It is this facility to 'benchmark' performances in managerial skills which is the missing link in much conventional management education and training.

A second generalization about this skills-based approach to performance-improvement is that the quality of learning required to deliver measurable improvements in the practice of a skill must be consistently high. Effective training now requires the provision of training material for both managers and staff which is finely tuned to the improvement of specific skills. Let us look at how this can be done.

Effective training delivery

In organizations where focused skills training is critical to the performance of organizations and to the quality of the products or services offered, a delivery system which can distribute training swiftly and accurately to people is a vital requirement of modern management practice. The supply of information to assist staff in the conduct of tasks, even those which appear routine and simplistic, has increased enormously. Yet it is in the treatment of apparently simple task performances that well-directed training can be most effective. Raising the awareness of an individual to the personal opportunities for challenge and skill in such tasks is a massively important part of an effective training programme.

The requirement for high-performance organizations to advance the skill deliveries of their managements is no less important. Here the choices available may be more complex, and will include directed self-study as well as residential training. Again, it is the paramount importance of intensifying the volume and the specificity of learning material available to the manager which demarcates self-study, or open learning, as a key instrument of effective training delivery.

Let us examine training delivery systems for both large groups of employees in more immediate job-related training situations, and for managers with responsibilities for the performance of departmental or business units.

Training for single skills performance

A training strategy seeking consistent performance improvements from employees will need to identify the primary skill requirement of each defined job. This can be more difficult than it looks. One problem is that jobs can be unwittingly de-skilled by over-simplification of the task, or under-skilled by setting performance requirements which lack lustre. There needs to be a clear identification of a core skill in each job, around which the main performance indicators can be expressed, and in terms of which the achievement of people can be set. Jobs which lack this characteristic are unlikely to command interest or provide more than minimal opportunity for human performance improvement.

A retailing example may be helpful here. A core retailing skill is selling a product to a customer. Even allowing for the scale of self-service purchasing by customers, the opportunity to sell products and the service of the business to the customer is manifest. Yet selling products and customer services, however important these activities rank in the priorities of organizations, are often assumed to be readily acquired by adults, requiring only superficial training and almost no reinforcement. Regrettably, these attitudes to selling remain commonplace. With such assumptions we can come to 'de-skill' the very jobs on which the survival of the organization depends.

In reality, selling is a transactional skill of some complexity requiring product knowledge, a selling technique, and an understanding of buying psychology. These elements can be organized into a framework of learning, and it is the command of such learning which enables the salesperson to grow in the skills of selling. We repeat, it is the primary purpose of effective training to communicate and transfer this sense of growth and achievement in the practice of a skill. Developing this sense in the salesperson as well as in the manager is the substance of all achieving cultures. Effective training is about the creation and maintenance of such cultures.

If people need to own skills and become multi-skilled, achieving organizations are based upon teams of 'achieving' people. As individual and team access to self-paced learning systems intensifies, so also should be the awareness of skill and of high competence in its delivery.

How technologically sophisticated these systems are is much less important than their ability to sustain the learning requirement of the individual, and to produce a measurable improvement in the performance of a skill. Paper-based systems are as valid as computer-based systems in this respect, and much less expensive. Selecting an appropriate training delivery system becomes more rigorous as the options available range from low to high-tech formats.

In larger organizations the opportunities to network skills training to workplaces become more cost-effective with the growth of communications infrastructures, and with the use of microcomputers in everyday business practice. Inevitably computer-based and video-linked training will become a key component of a flexible delivery strategy which might also include paper-based and face-to-face systems of training.

Indeed, effective training functions will possess a capability to select appropriate delivery systems for differing performance needs with accuracy and confidence. The choice and cost of delivery will depend on the scale and urgency of the need. We can illustrate this by looking again at a core skill of retailing: selling.

To present to salespersons the challenge and skill of effective selling requires a sequence which will include the following elements:

- identifying the sales orientation of the salesperson;
- recognizing the purchasing styles of customers;
- exercising and developing the skills of recognition, interpretation, and evaluation of sales transactions, and
- selecting the right skills to manage the transaction competently.

Practising this sequence forms the basis of a skilled activity, one which can be consciously managed by the salesperson, and which can be worked and re-worked with increasing confidence as performance improves. It follows that the power of the delivery system and its technology must be sufficient to assist learning and skill development accurately and to the standard required.

In high-performance organizations a powerful delivery system will include the following elements:

- an appropriate technology: paper-, computer-based training; paper-, computer-linked to video, videotext, videodisc, etc.;
- a student guide to the system: details of objectives, method, structure and routing of the system;
- an appropriate structure: modules, segments, sections;
- an acceptable method of assessing performance;
- a process of providing critical feedback to the student, and
- a service of tutorial support.

Any plan for human achievement in organizations in the mid-eighties and onwards seems likely to incorporate a training strategy that includes delivery systems capable of streaming learning to people in workplaces for the primary purpose of skill development and improved performance. This capability to enrich work by paced skill development is the primary contribution of training to improved business performance.

Training for multi-skills performance

When we turn to management training and its requirements for multi-skills development, the real potential of performance-related training becomes evident. Here the approach is to define management activities in terms of its key skills, using a methodology which allows for high specificity in skill definitition. This methodology has been described already in the chapter. Here, we can say something about the follow-up training to profiling.

Identifying training needs in the way we have described already provides a powerful incentive for the student to correct an identified weakness as quickly as possible. Further, we can show that individual training needs in management are much narrower than is generally believed. Indeed, when one concentrates on a skills approach to management development, specific needs can be identified with precision. Finally, we can show that the skills themselves fall into two major categories. In the first are people-management, and inter-personal skills which can best be developed through interactive training on residential courses. In the second category are analytical, cognitive skills which are amenable to learning by self-study, or open learning.

The development of multi-skills management performance depends on devising a suitable mix of interactive and analytical learning programmes.

At the end of each skill development programme, a final exercise should be offered to the student as the basis on which a measured improvement in skill performance can be determined.

CONCLUSION

In this chapter we have considered the following aspects of effective training management:

1   linking human resource development strategies with business strategies;
2   creating a performance-orientated human resource development programme, and

3 designing and delivering a performance-related training programme.

Effective training management begins with an awareness by the organization that the performance development of its human resources is directly geared to the development of the business of the organization. Sustained business improvement cannot occur without sustained resourcing of people.

Effective training management requires, above all, the preparation and regular updating of an organization training plan. It is in this plan that the development priorities of managers and managed as human resources can be set out, reviewed, and renewed in an ongoing training cycle. In this way, the development of people is always phased to reflect the priorities of skilled development required to advance the business of the organization.

Effective training management requires this kind of recognition from those who direct the strategy of the organization. In achieving organizations, human resource planning is used to give the business a competitive advantage. Developing people to build, manage, and advance the performance of organizations is the real purpose of an effective training function.

CHECKLIST

The main steps to managing an effective training function are as follows:

1 Define a 'people' strategy, or a human resources development strategy within the business strategy of the organization.
2 Define the role of training within the HRD strategy, i.e. create a training strategy.
3 Focus the training strategy on performance-related training, i.e. training geared to the measured improvement of core skills.
4 Create a focused learning response to individual skills profiling. This response to provide a mixed-media range of learning and exercising.
5 Create a company training infra-structure owned by the organization, and not by the trainers.

REFERENCES/FUTURE READING

Practical advice on effective management is available from many sources, not just those concerned directly with the management of the training and development function. Here we provide a selection of those sources available, some of which have been drawn upon in the preparation of this chapter.

Managing the T & D function

Bennett, R. (ed.), *'Get in There'* – *Managing the Business of Training*, five workbooks from Trainer Support Services, UK, 1986 (see particularly Workbook 2 – Business Needs and Plans, by Bennett and Laidlaw, and Workbook 4 – Managing for Success, by Jeremy Spoor).

Camp, R.R. et al, *Toward a More Effective Training Strategy and Practice*, Prentice-Hall Inc., Engelwood Cliffs, New Jersey, 1986.

Pepper, A.D., *Managing the Training and Development Function*, Gower, 1984.

Walker, J.W. (ed.), *The Challenge of Human Resource Planning: Selected Readings*. Human Resource Planning Society, pp. 101–111, 1979.

Managing generally

Armstrong, A., *How to be a Better Manager*, Kogan Page, London, 1983.

Bennett, R., *Managing Personnel and Performance* – *An Alternative Approach*, Business Books, London, 1981.

Brodie, M. and Bennett, R. (eds), *Perspectives on Managerial Effectiveness*, Thamesman Publications, 1979.

Hunningher, Erica (ed.), *The Manager's Handbook* – *The Practical Guide to Successful Management*, Arthur Young, 1986.

Other sources

Bowen, P., *Social Control in Industrial Organisations*, Routledge and Kegan Paul, London (Chapter 3, pp. 57–77 and Chapter 10, pp. 242–253 on 'balance' and 'contract' between organizations and their memberships), 1976.

Churchill, G.A. et al., The Determinants of Salesperson Performance: A Meta-Analysis, *Journal of Marketing Research*, vol. xxii, May, pp. 103–118, 1985.

Davis, H.L. and Silk, A.J., Interaction and Influence Processes in Personal Selling: *Sloan Management Review*, vol. 13, no. 2, pp. 59–76, 1972.

Futrell, C.M., *ABC's of Selling*, Irwin. Chapter 2, pp. 49–71, 1980.

9 The Career Dimension

Julian Davies and John Burgoyne

In this chapter we outline some of the issues concerned with the trainers' careers.

In particular we emphasize the importance of trainers being concerned about their own career and development as professionals. This is an area in which too often in the past trainers have not practised what they exorted others to do. This has had, as we shall point out, serious implications for the influence and effectiveness of training departments.

In our research into the careers of trainers one important relationship we observed was that between the career concepts of trainers and the strategy adopted by training departments towards their main clients. This relationship is not always recognized, and is likely in some situations to become self-reinforcing. This, as we shall show, has serious implications for the continued existence of the training function in a particular context.

Finally in this chapter we look at some of the present changes in the way training is organized and the impact these changes are having on trainers' careers. This examination will lead us to re-emphasize and reinforce our initial concern that trainers are too often unaware of the importance of investing in their own development and of managing their own careers.

The reason why we focus on trainers' careers is that we see training as an activity which is dependent for its effectiveness on the trainers who manage, design and implement a training event. Attempts to see training as 'pure' development or education of a receptive group of trainees have often failed to recognize the importance of the human role in implementing training. For example, recent work on distance learning has again emphasized the importance of a trainer/tutor helping learning to take place.

The research underlying this chapter has been carried out in the United Kingdom, and some of the phenomena we describe are related to specific UK institutions, such as the Manpower Services Commission and Industrial Training Boards. However, we think it likely that the main features and the underlying framework of our argument will have more general applicability.

Other studies of trainers have concentrated on their role and their particular skills and competencies. In this chapter we want to draw on our work on the careers of trainers in order to emphasize that the way in which a trainer carries out his role is related to his past, present and future jobs, and in particular to his career concept as a trainer. Our view of career starts from a supposition that it is concerned with the interaction between an individual and his environment, that career paths are constantly changing, reflecting changes both in the individual and environment – both of the organizational context as well as the wider influences of economic, social and technical change. The research on which this chapter is based was carried out in the early 1980s, a time of change in the UK's 'professional training environment' with the abolition of the Industrial Training Boards, the growth of youth training courses, and the increased power of the Manpower Services Commission as against the Department of Education and Science. Organizations in the private manufacturing sector in particular were feeling the full effects of recession – many faced with financial pressures reduced their training departments, other put pressure on trainers to run different types of courses and trainers were asked to justify their existence, as training was no longer viable as a 'prestige' activity.

All this turmoil had a continuing impact on the careers of individual trainers. However, as careers are experienced at an individual level the effect of the impact varied, and for many this period was one of reaction to outside forces rather than a proactive approach towards managing their own career development. This is one of the paradoxical themes running through this chapter, that trainers despite being in the 'business' of training and developing others are not practising what they preach. Indeed, the ideas of managing their own careers and development are often not even considered either by themselves or by those who manage the training function.

This lack of self-management has wider implications than a concern for the effective development of individuals: it is also related to the wider issue of the relationship between training and the context it seeks to influence. In a sense, influence depends on many factors, of which power and its credible use is one; knowledge, and control of that knowledge, is one source of power. However, if trainers have not considered what their source of knowledge and power is, how to develop it, what type of activities and roles they should undertake, then their competency is not fully used. Thus their influence and effectiveness is likely to be less than if they were more active in developing and managing their own careers. 'Managing' in this context is less about control and one fixed set of professional patterns, and more concerned with understanding an individual's career path and the underlying career concept.

One of the themes of this chapter will be the flexibility of trainers' careers, which at one extreme can be the ultimate in opportunism and luck, and at the other extreme can be an understood and managed pragmatism. This pragmatism, like contingency management style, takes into account the training needs of a student and the strengths and weaknesses of the trainer concerned in order to provide an effective match.

CAREER PATHS

One way of exploring career-related issues for trainers is to look at the chronology of their career development, how they came to be trainers, what skills and competencies they develop while in training, their identification with training, the career concepts they develop, and what other jobs they move to after training.

First, the idea of a career is problematical for many trainers, as even safe niches become affected by an increasingly turbulent environment. Many trainers ironically feel threatened by having to develop new skills and knowledge not only in the training context but also having to move out of training into the wider organizational context. In the past training and trainers have too often been isolated from the mainstream of the organizational life.

Trainers have been happy to develop their own professional competence, often in isolation from changing organizational and managerial needs. They have been seen as a homogeneous group by those involved in developing their job-specific skills. The wide range of career concepts and identities described in this chapter are not always recognized.

Indeed, to many outside training, training departments and the staff in them are regarded as unusual, as being in an 'ivory tower' and 'divorced from reality'. This myth continues, fuelled by ignorance and by the fact that there is only a limited movement of people between training and line management.

An understanding of some of the aspects of trainers' careers is necessary before this myth can be challenged effectively. First of all, career paths are very variable; there is no one entry route, trainers are recruited from a variety of jobs and bring different skills and understanding to their job.

This variety is relevant and important as trainers, to be effective, should not be an isolated 'elite' but should be integrated into organizational concerns. One form of integration is through shared experiences, and the wider the past jobs from which trainers come the more likely they are, within a particular organization, to be able to meet trainee demands for face credibility and understanding.

Trainers themselves see the process of entry into training as confused, a combination of negative pressures, a stalemate in their previous job, lack of advancement (especially for non-management trainers) together with a specific encouragement from their boss or a trainer resulting in a decision to try training. The selection process is two-way, as managers of the training functions also have their view of what is an appropriate background for a trainer. Again, the selection process is not always clear cut and may involve looking for people with similar rather than complementary backgrounds, both in terms of content and the organization. So for example many functional trainers such as craft or specialist trainers spend their career in one organization and often they are selected for their specific background.

Management trainers are likely to come from a more diverse background and emphasis is placed on the less concrete process skills which cannot so easily be related to specific past job titles and roles. Management trainers' work requires them to deal with senior managers, and some organizations deal with this by recruiting from outside the organization, particularly when 'setting up' or changing the role of a management training department.

As well as having more diverse entry patterns, the management trainers were also less organizationally-based and more willing to move across organizations. This was partly a function of their background being in more generalized conceptual areas rather than organization or job-specific activities. Also management training is less tangible than other types of training and less obviously related to immediate business needs and the continuing existence of the organization. This tends to make management training more marginal in many organizations and usually the section is relatively small, making promotion prospects in management training sections more restricted. Yet for individuals there is a greater variety in career identities open to trainers. This variety, while providing individual opportunities for personal growth and job satisfaction, also brings with it the danger of becoming isolated and divorced from the wider environment in which training functions.

TRAINING AS DEVELOPMENT

There are three main ways in which a time in training is seen as a development process. First, for a few a spell in training is specifically linked with future career development; second, there is the development of specific trainer skills and competencies; and third there is the process of development arising from the role and function of the training department.

The first type of development is an exception to the usual serendipitous approach to selection, and indicates the way in which a brief time in training can be used as a rite of passage to transform individuals from non-managerial to managerial roles. Particular examples of this are sales training where individual salespeople come into training for a short time, around two to three years, as preparation for a future career as a manager of the sales function. It is also the practice of some companies to move people from the shop floor to supervisor via a spell as an instructor in the training department. The promotion is explicitly to instructor/supervisor, and the period in training is again limited to two to three years.

An increasing use of this type of short-term period in training is that of secondment as a way of personally developing an individual usually not linked to promotion. However, the fixed period in training does seem to have a rejuvenating or reawakening effect on previously moribund careers.

Such types of explicit career development are not the norm. However, where they occur they provide an important link between the training department and its clients. In many ways, despite the disruption and lack of professional skills of people on secondment, their contribution in terms of an exchange of information and their future ambassadorial role for training is very significant.

The second type of development already referred to is that of specific trainer skills. It is usually seen as an organizational necessity to ensure that all new entrants reach a certain level of ability to train the clients of the department. Thus new entrants are quickly socialized into the 'survival skills' current in that department. There are two problems to this approach; first, too many initial instructor training courses tend towards a static and non-developmental view of training. This is compounded by the fact that for many trainers it is their first and last experience of formal training and development, and in the absence of any other development experiences they can continue to repeat their first year's experience for periods of up to twenty years.

Second, this approach to socializing the new entrant into the trainer role can sidestep the option of using the fresh perspective of the newcomer to develop new approaches and priorities in training.

Development patterns of trainers, either through formal or informal on-the-job development of new projects and roles, are difficult to identify. There is the paradox of a function having the role of developing and training others, and yet only rarely being introspective in terms of consciously developing and training its own members. So in most cases there appears to be a random pattern of attending courses unrelated to individual or organizational needs; even when training programmes do exist formal schemes and patterns of development do not necessarily provide an answer. What turns out to be most helpful is the recommendation of a particular event by a colleague or boss.

Yet despite the lack of introspection, trainers and extrainers identified the time they had put into training as being one of great development for them as individuals. Especially in terms of the wide non-specific skills connected with personal relationship, and in the increased knowledge of particular courses and subjects. Particularly, they stressed that they had developed a qualitative change in their perspective on management, organizational goals and policies.

Training brought them into contact with most aspects and functions of the organization and through this they broadened their perspective from a narrow functional view to one which encompassed complex interrelationships and connected them to the overall purpose of organizational goals.

For many, the contact with central senior managers also made them more aware of trends in the business and associated changing attitudes and behaviour patterns. Being in training increased their visibility and knowledge of the informal system in the organization and in some cases, because of the physical situation of training, gave a close proximity to decision-making centres. However, with some exceptions it did not seem possible for trainers to 'cash in' on this visibility and contact; that is, trainers were not seen as potential recruits to management posts in most organizations. Despite having developed a broader knowledge of how the organization worked, they were perceived as being too specialized.

CAREER CONCEPTS

The development opportunities of a time in training are perceived and acted upon differently by individuals. One of the important discoveries of our research was the link between trainers' career concepts and the way in which the training departments they worked in related to their host organizations.

The study of careers is connected with the identity of an individual in a particular role. As such this identity is very sensitive to changes in the environment and the organizational context. Thus a focus on careers of trainers provides an insight into the relationship between a training department and the organization it seeks to influence.

As has already been stressed this relationship is a dynamic one, as is the concept of a career. Within any one career there are also changes of career identity and entry into training provides one such change.

In our categorization of career identities we found that it was not the time which people spent in training which helped them develop their identity, but rather their understanding and commitment to the process and wider purposes of training.

Non-Trainer anchored career identities

Content based
Organization based
Hierarchical career progressions

Trainer anchored career identities

Mobile specialist
Expert
Actor
Personal development
Developer of others
Missionary

Figure 9:1   Categorization of career concepts of direct trainers

Figure 9:1 shows our categorization of career identitites for trainers. They break down first of all into the two major categories of those which are not particularly to do with the training process, and those which are.

In the first category we found three 'identities'. The first is the *content based* trainer, whose primary identity is based on some topic, skill, or expertise in which he is an expert, and who happens to be applying that expertise by training others in it. Such expertise is often, but not always, technological, and the person would tend to be as happy applying the technology, selling it, providing customer technical support, doing research and development on or with it, as he or she is in training in it. The *organization based* person is the company man or woman who rotates round a number of jobs in the same organization, and does a spell in training. Such people are perhaps found to be valuable in training because they 'know the ropes', and can socialize trainees into the ways of the company. The *hierarchical career progression* category refers to those who are concerned to 'get on' in a conventional career sense of climbing a status ladder, and find training a useful career step for this purpose. We have found this pattern in traditional industrial contexts where operator $\rightarrow$ trainer $\rightarrow$ foreman $\rightarrow$ supervisor is the route, and also in professional fields such as social work and in the transition from sales to sales management.

The other six trainer identities are more rooted in the training role itself. The *mobile specialist* is someone whose career is based round a training speciality, such as safety, or customer relations, or book-keeping, and moves job within and between organizations, or maybe as a freelance trainer, dealing with situations where needs for their kind of training arise. The *expert trainer* is someone whose career is based around some kind of expertise in the training process itself, like instructional techniques. Such a person is likely to stay close to the coal face of training, though the content, purpose and context of their training may change. The *actor* is someone whose career is rooted in a preference for performing in front of people, and we found a surprising number of these in training, including several who were in a literal sense explicitly frustrated actors. Those who were based in *personal development* were those who had had some quite significant experience of personal development and growth, often as a result of being a 'trainee', and were oriented to work that kept them in touch with this process and allowed them to make it happen for others. *Developers of others* were those whose work was oriented around a wish to work with and help others through the medium of training and teaching. This career actor was sometimes, but not always, associated with a belief that people need saving from the narrowing influences of work and organizational life. Finally, *missionaries* were those who had some cause or definite view of how people, the world, organizations or work should be and whose career pattern and choices derived from this view or belief.

We found that the last three of these categories – personal development, developer of others and missionary – intermingled, with individuals appearing to be based in one, but with strands of the other two.

There is a basic interaction between the way in which trainers see and experience their own career identity and the way in which they see the purpose and direction of training in an organizational context. Being an interaction there are changes over time, but like all systems there is a tendency towards stasis: in order to keep the interaction alive a career has to be actively managed.

A trainer's career identity has implications for the way in which training is delivered and managed. In particular the ability of training to be a source of influence in a particular context will depend on how trainers operate and also how they understand their own career identity. So some trainers are primarily concerned with individual development both of themselves and of others in terms of knowledge and personal understanding. Other trainers are concerned primarily with responding to stated organizational needs for particular types of training, and in Pettigrew's model are in the passive provider role. In many cases their career identity is organizationally based, or they may have an actor identity not so much concerned with questioning the outcome of a particular training event as with emphasizing the delivery of training sessions.

A final group of trainers may be concerned with a more active role in influencing the organization either by facilitating change or through operating as change agents. We have categorized these as missionaries. A fuller description of career concepts can be found in Davies and Burgoyne (1984).

CAREER CONCEPTS AND TRAINING IN ITS ORGANIZATIONAL CONTEXT

In our research four main boundary management strategies were identified and associated with them were particular career concepts of trainers. These are outlined in Figure 9.2.

Boundary management strategy	Associated career concepts
Isolation	Personal development, content based, hierarchical status
Steady state	Actor, content, organization based, expert
Facilitation of change	Missionary, actor, developer of others, expert
Change agent	Missionary, organization based, mobile specialist

Figure 9.2   Relationships between career concepts and boundary management strategies

These four different strategies, often implicit, by which training functions relate to their host organizations, can be described as follows.

Training isolation

In the past this was quite a common strategy, although it is becoming increasingly non-viable as situations change. It can be recognized by the way in which trainers focus on internal matters and on internally decided criteria of good professional practice. Little attention is paid to trainers' views of how this is experienced, and the emphasis is on an elite group who know what is good for others. Often this situation of isolation is not recognized by the trainers, although symptoms such as increased difficulty in finding clients for courses and in getting organizational recognition begin to ring alarm bells.

Many of the trainers in such a function have been there a long time, and any new blood brought in is either assimilated or moves on very quickly.

The career concepts connected with this situation are those

belonging to trainers whose identities are about their own development, whether process, content, or status linked.

Steady state situation

Here the boundary between training and the organization is more permeable, and often symbiotic as training is closely linked to the existing organizational needs of the host culture. Trainers see themselves as being responsive and reactive to organizational requests for training, rather than questioning the relevance of these requests or suggesting alternative ways of meeting them. The close interrelationship between training and the task structure of the organization makes it relatively easy for people to enter training for a short time and return to jobs in the mainstream of the organization.

Career concepts associated with this relationship are those connected with the organizational and content bases. Trainer identities are more difficult to develop as the training process tends to be devalued or not regarded as an important element. So trainers with specialist skills are not developed due to time pressures and the general questionable nature of a specialist career. Those that do exist are trainers with an actor or expert identity.

Facilitation of change

Here the boundary is more actively managed by the training function, although the close relationship of the steady state is absent. There is greater stress on the professionalism of trainers who are required to have a high credibility in organizational terms in order to persuade managers to change.

Movement of trainers in and out of the department is limited, except for a minority who come in for short periods, sometimes to provide a particular expert content or for their own development.

The trainer identities particularly associated with this situation are the missionary, and the actor who is important for front credibility and acceptance. The missionary, however, faces particular problems of being stuck in a long-term role, which after a ten-year period becomes increasingly unsatisfying. Yet, despite developing skills and abilities, trainers in this situation are too identified with a specialism to be easily transferable to another organizational context.

Change agent

In this strategy trainers seek to break down the boundaries between training and the organization. The flow is seen as being two-way but is initiated by the trainer, who takes his identity into the organization. In order to manage this situation a clear purpose is needed about the impact that training should make on the organization. How this impact is made will be more through consulting, tailor-made events, counselling, and on the job projects, and less through direct courses.

This type of training can be very demanding in terms of process and skills. The Trainer with an actor identity is less likely to be effective in this rapidly changing situation. Whereas those with a more developmental identity can find satisfaction and short-term success, longer-term success and acceptance is reliant on linking individual needs to organizational development. The success of this training strategy is closely related to the career identities of the trainers, and the skills and approaches they have developed. In order to initiate this process training departments sometimes bring in outside professional specialists who, having established the strategy, can then leave the implementation to trainers recruited from within the organization.

WHERE DO EXPERIENCED TRAINERS MOVE TO?

As has been described in detail, this varies from the trainers' perspective according to the contract at the start of entry into training, the career concepts of individuals, and the development experience of the individuals involved. The organizational perspective is also relevant, as the boundary management strategy of the training department will influence the extent to which a trainer can return to a 'mainstream' organizational role. Thus the role of a trainer and the role of the training function are both influenced by and influence the career of a trainer. However, from an individual perspective there are certain aspects to be aware of in terms of making decisions on future career plans.

One aspect which affects all trainers is that of the job cycle and time period in training. The timing of an individual's career path is often neglected. The 'seductive' nature of the job itself and the opportunities for self development (already mentioned and described in more detail in the following sections) blind individuals to the passing of time. The management of the careers of trainers is a neglected issue leading to multiple problems for individuals, the training function and the organization(s) which are its clients. An outline of the job cycles in training is illustrated in Figure 9.3.

Phase	Time Period	
Entry	1 week to 9 months	Induction period
	2½ years	Coping with the job
Contribution	2½ years to 7 years	Contribution to new development in training
Exit	3 years to 5 years	Optimum time for change of job
	7 years	Plateauing of satisfaction in training
'Stuck'	10 years	Dissatisfaction, 'stuck' in a routine

Figure 9:3   Timing of job cycles in training

This aspect of job cycles is not unique to training, nor are career transitions and moves from functions to general management. However, what is significant from a training perspective is the difference in value placed on a time in training; non-trainers view it as a fallow time in which an individual is out of touch with the mainstream of organizational life while trainers have almost the opposite perspective of having gained a much more central view of an organization. Indeed sometimes politically they may 'see' too much for their own good and become a danger to the organization.

So what happens to trainers after a period in training? Where do they move to? Some obviously don't move, and remain in the same department being passed over, becoming dissatisfied and contributing to the myth of training as a dumping ground. One important aspect influencing their movement is their career concept as shown in Figure 9.1. For example, trainers with hierarchical perspectives get promoted and become managers of trainers, and in a few cases managers of the personnel function.

Organizational movement within the training function is possible for many trainers, particularly those who are mobile specialists and experts who are continually moving between organizations. Indeed that movement is part of their 'stock in trade' and needs to continue if they are to continue to develop their competence effectively. Content-based trainers may also move, but usually for promotion or because of negative pressures rather than as a positive career move. In their case content itself is the development vehicle and the process and context of training are irrelevant or unimportant. Problems become evident here when the content itself becomes obsolete and outdated, as is increasingly happening due to the wider changes not only of technology but also of the economy and society. Although outside this focus, such changes are occurring most acutely in those educational establishments where teachers derive their expertise from content.

The other groups of trainer-anchored career identities are those of the actor and development concepts. The actor identity is one which relies on personal performance and having the right stage, in that sense it is possible for such a trainer to switch organizations and contexts effectively as long as the job requires a performance rather than consulting, facilitation or development of others. However, since for an actor the satisfaction is in the actual training arena they may not wish to move from a particular setting and so may in effect block training posts and reduce the effectiveness of the training function.

As regards trainers who have development career concepts, the personal development road is increasingly one which leads out of organizational constraints into roles independent of organizations. As this is an area of growth in some terms, e.g. independent consultants, it provides an avenue for career development. However, it is also a precarious and changing role in which market forces determine the requests made of a trainer. Demands can change rapidly, and trainers need to be aware of the importance of monitoring their own development.

In fact one of the trends in management training is that of the growth of the independent consultant role both in voluntary and involuntary terms. In the 1970s much emphasis in management development literature was on the need to recognize the decline of stable work and career patterns for managers. Organizations, it was prophesied, would be increasingly employing experts and professionals on short-term contracts, there would be an increase in independent experts selling their expertise and working from their own homes.

The core of organizationally employed staff would diminish and a lifelong organizational career would be a rarity. This development has now occurred in the training and particularly the management training field.

CHANGES IN THE ORGANIZATION AND DELIVERY OF TRAINING

A number of factors have contributed to this growth and change, for individuals their influence will obviously vary as it has in their previous decision to enter training.

First, for some there is the negative pressure ranging from individual redundancy to the reduction of a training function from a sizeable group of ten to one person who is the manager of training and who buys in courses, to the removal of a whole training establishment. In particular one important impact was that of the rundown of the UK's Industrial Training Boards. This was not just significant for trainers employed in the Boards. There was also an effect on training departments which had relied on the levy grant system to justify their existence; this has meant that many people's careers have been abruptly ended and they have had to look for new areas and new jobs in which to work. For others the negative pressure becomes an opportunity for personal development and change so that redundancy is proactively sought for the opportunity it brings with it, together with the opportunity of being free from the constraints of undertaking work which is the choice of others.

This growth is supported by changes in the wider environment; in particular there is a growing 'macro-culture' of 'entrepreneurship', a stress on the importance of the individual, and the role and acceptability to the market economy which provides an appropriate climate for the development of a small business enterprise. Even when the management trainers actively espouse other values in their work they can in terms of their own development operate as training entrepreneurs.

Finally there is a growing market for independent expertise; private organizations recognize the benefits of a reduced workforce and of decentralization. Many are selling or have sold their large training centres and so have less concern about filling beds and justifying costs by numbers trained.

Public organizations are under a different kind of pressure to reduce the numbers employed for political and economic reasons, and to provide more responsive and less monolithic and all-embracing programmes. In many cases they find it difficult to recruit people with the right potential and skills from within the organization. Yet training managers cannot afford, nor would it be politically or economically possible, to buy in on a full-time basis.

Thus they are developing a strategic approach to buying in selective training expertise, being willing to pay for such expertise, and using it in specific contexts and for particular purposes yet not having to pay the hidden full-time costs of employing and using such expertise or having to develop and find re-employment for 'burnt out' trainers.

Such developments have a symbiotic character for both organizations and trainers, although the risks are borne largely by the trainers since organizations are free to try out and discard consultants as the needs change. As yet it is difficult to forecast the lifespan of consultants; much depends on their career concepts, their willingness to invest in their own development and their physical and emotional stamina in working as individuals in different locations. One development is the growth of consulting organizations and the transformation of accounting and audit firms into homes for groups of consultants, thus providing some support but perhaps not guaranteeing lifelong employment.

Another development in the area of trainer employment is that of the growth of youth training schemes which have again provided employment, if only on a year-to-year basis for ex-Industry Training Board trainers, unemployed teachers and those working on the development of others. These together with other MSC funded schemes provide an organizational base for non-management trainees and an opportunity to develop new skills. However, the transitory and fragmented nature of many of the schemes may cause problems for individuals. Nevertheless, the development of approaches to develop the skills of trainers and managers of these schemes is hopeful, although these cannot replace the in-depth development of training which took place in some organizations before the 1980s. What then are the future careers of trainers likely to be?

CONCLUSIONS

The patterns of trainers' careers reflect the twin theories of change and development at an individual, organizational, and environmental level. As trainers are concerned with these issues as part of their task the impact on them of these changes reflects complex dynamics, for trainers themselves have a potential role in influencing the direction and speed of some organizational changes.

Moreover it is possible for trainers to be more proactive in managing their own careers. Managing is used here in the sense of understanding and influencing their own career. The idea of managing as a static control concept is increasingly redundant as an approach to trainers' careers. The growth of professionalization and accreditation may not be the answer to the flexible and dynamic nature of trainers' careers. The skills and competencies trainers need to develop are less about static or knowledge-based approaches, and more about the development of new approaches, new roles, and new career paths. In one sense the growth of the independent consultant is an aspect of this in which the evaluation of success does not rely on having been accredited, but is related to the clients' recognition of expertise and competency. This does raise the question of the role of the outside trainer in meeting multiple stakeholders' needs and actually influencing organizations to change and develop. In terms of training strategies, isolation is increasingly being challenged, the steady state role is diminishing as managers begin to respond to a turbulent environment.

In conclusion, if trainers in any role are to operate as facilitators of change and development, being reflexive about their own development is a priority. It is more than being consistent in practising on oneself what one preaches to others, it is a necessary strategy both for individual careers and for the role of training as an effective influence on ways of operating and managing.

One way of summing up this chapter from a practical point of view is to highlight some questions that *trainers* and *managers of trainers* might try to answer, and consider whether their answers call for any action (see Figure 9.4, overleaf).

For Trainers	For Managers of Trainers/ Training Departments/ Trainers' Careers
What is my career concept? content organization career progress mobile specialist training expert actor personal development developer of others missionary Am I working in an organizational situation compatible with my career concept? Am I in the right job? Am I doing it right? What future career moves fitting my career concept are open to me? Am I/should I/can I influence the orientation of the training department/function I am in? What are the implications of all this for my own development?	What is the 'boundary management' of my unit/sector/department, etc.? Is this as it should be? Do I have training staff with career concepts compatible with my actual or intended strategy? Are there viable career paths for my trainees, both within and beyond my unit? Is there anything I should be doing in the way of career facilitation and counselling? Where am I up to on 'training the trainers' in the light of the above? What about myself in terms of all the questions for trainers on the left?

Figure 9:4

REFERENCES/FURTHER READING

Source material for chapter

Davies, J. and Burgoyne, J.G., *Career Paths of Direct Trainers*, MSC, June 1984.

Davies, J., 'Patterns and Paradoxes of Trainers' Careers: the Implications for the Influences of Training', *JEIT Monograph*, vol. 9, no. 2, 1985.

Relevant other studies

Bennett, R., and Leduchowicz, T., 'What Makes for an Effective Trainer', *JEIT Monograph*, vol. 7, no. 2, 1983.

Pettigrew, A., Jones, G., and Reason, P., 'Training and Development Roles in their Organizational Setting', in *MSC Training Studies*, October, 1982.

Distance learning

Harris, W.J.A., 'The Distance Tutor Education by Correspondence' in *Manchester Monograph 3*, 1975.

Hodgson V., 'Distance Learning in Management Education' in *Journal of Innovative Higher Education*, vol. 2, no. 1, 1985.

Job cycles and career patterns generally

Handy, C., *Understanding Organizations*, Penguin, Harmondsworth 1976.

James, K., 'The Development of Senior Managers for the Future' in Beck J., and Cox C., (eds.), *Advance in Management Education*, Wiley, Chichester 1980.

Katz, R., 'Managing Careers: the Influence of Job and Group Longevities' in Katz R., (ed.), *Career Issues in Human Resource Management*, Prentice-Hall, Englewood Cliffs, New Jersey, 1982.

10 The Cultural Context
Phillip Wright

During the last decade, especially since the publication of Pascale and Athos' book *The Art of Japanese Management* in 1981, the way in which North Americans and Europeans manage their organizations has come under intense scrutiny. Much of this interest has been generated by our perceived failure to compete with aggressive far eastern economies and by a general, undefined malaise that appears to affect our entire industrial/public sector structure.

Many of our business and industrial inadequacies are said to result from out-moded management techniques that have created dysfunctional cultures. Cultures are reported to contain the root causes of our recent managerial decline in that the notion of corporate culture addresses the real human issues that often impinge on the success of an organization. It has been suggested that culture can anaesthetize leaders against problems that, from the outside, are painfully obvious. None of these ideas are new, yet little has been done to integrate the theoretical concepts of corporate or organizational culture into the mainstream of training practice. As we have seen in Chapter 2 however, the 'culture' of an organization has been shown by research to have a considerable influence on trainer effectiveness.

Although it has been suggested that the study of corporate culture is an 'inexact' or 'pseudo-science', there is a general commonality of definition. Campbell (1984), for example, defines corporate culture as 'the attitudes, values, beliefs and expectations of those who work in an organization', while Pascale (1984) indicates that culture is 'a set of shared values, norms and beliefs that get (sic) everybody heading in the same direction'. Similarly, Field and Davies (1984) refer to the 'behaviour patterns and standards that bind it (the organization) together' and to Drake (1984), culture is 'a set of values and beliefs shared by people working in an organization'.

The common attributes then, are values, beliefs and attitudes that somehow are shared. These organizational characteristics can be functional or dysfunctional, but each organization will have a culture that bears strongly on its success, or even on its survival.

THE MULTI-LEVEL CULTURE CONCEPT AS A VEHICLE FOR TRAINING

The training professional should look at corporate, or organizational culture (for the same phenomena are found in public sector organizations) as having three main pillars or facets – philosophy, activities and systems (Figure 10:1). Indeed, the trainer who is aware of the constantly unfolding cultural panorama in which he/she works and can respond to it at all levels, is in a position to make a valuable contribution to organizational objectives.

Philosophy

The development of a management philosophy is central to the creation of a functional corporate culture. Of primary importance is the attitude of top-level management, as it is here that the necessary unifying philosophy and spirit originates. For example, the frequently used phrase referring to the 'family feeling' at Delta Airlines is attributed to a policy of open door access to management, a feeling of caring and the President's attitude that one doesn't just join a company, one joins an 'objective'. This attitude leads to the conscious cultivation of internal guidance systems by impressing basic values and beliefs, thus reducing the need for external bureaucratic controls.

The process of developing internally motivated employees must begin with a strategic plan. Indeed, it should incorporate senior management's desire to build the necessary cultural

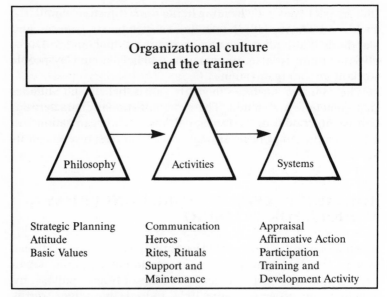

Figure 10:1   The multi-level culture concept

Note: Adapted and presented with permission from the Canadian Institute of Management.

infrastructure into the very foundation of the organization. Strategic planning does not end with a definition of purpose and general corporate direction, but continues on to develop the general philosophy of how individuals will be treated and managed throughout their working lives. Without constant, visible support and encouragement, senior management will lose control of an organization's cultural direction, for organizations are constantly changing in response to a multitude of internal and external forces. This inevitable evolution either can be managed or left to chance – the choice is up to the senior management team.

The design of an overall high level strategy is the first step in creating a viable organizational culture. The development of a corporate management philosophy could be the most important determinant of a firm's success or failure.

The cultural profile – Preparation for training and development

At this level, the trainer's main function is in the preparation of a cultural profile that will help to guide management in the cultural creation process, especially as it concerns the development and training of the human resource. According to Dr Homer Hagedorn (1984), a consultant with the prestigious Arthur D. Little Company, a profile is 'the most candid statement possible of what a company stands for and what it can't stand'. In order to obtain the profile, he advocates a procedure based on a 'systematic' interviewing technique consisting of open-ended questions, so that a 'sample of experts' can be polled concerning their perceptions of the organization's characteristics. These people are asked both direct – 'What does the company do best?' – and 'evocative' questions: 'If you remember the founder of the company, what sort of person was he, and what did he expect of people?' With some practice, the answer can help to isolate 'internal patterns that are unique to a particular company' or organization. It has been found that by identifying the 'prudent warrior', i.e., an experienced survivor, a list of 'critical symptoms' can be tabulated. Organizations, then, can 'audit' their cultures just as they would audit other aspects of the business.

A specific example concerns an audit, performed within a public sector organization, that stemmed from two isolated incidents. The first, was a comment by a former associate who, when entering a virtually empty open-concept office declared: 'things sure have changed. When I was here you could walk in at 5:00 p.m. and still find all the employees sitting around talking. Look, it's only 4 o'clock and the place looks like an empty barn!' The second incident involved one of the original group of employees hired by the organization. Conversations with this individual determined that he left after more than ten years because he found it an 'unpleasant place in which to work'. These two incidents suggested that the working environment had become less fulfilling. Through the development of a 'cultural profile', therefore, it was hoped to provide valuable insight into the contemporary culture. Only after the characteristics of the culture were understood could viable attempts be made to adjust it.

The audit process began by determining the factors that characterize an ideal workplace. The plan was to compare the present work situation with these data and then to determine where improvements could be made.

It was found that the 'ideal' culture would have all of the following characteristics:

1   a unifying philosophy and spirit emanating from top management,
2   the conscious cultivation of internal guidance systems by inculcating basic values and beliefs,
3   intensive initiation into the culture,
4   the provision of regular, positive feedback,
5   intense communications,
6   encouragement of internal competition,
7   allowance for mistakes,
8   the use of 'heroes' or role models, rites and rituals,
9   work is given meaning through a general emphasis or orientation on caring and on people rather than the mechanistic side of management,
10 sound human resources management systems
    - adequate pay and benefits,
    - fair appraisal procedures,
    - affirmative action programmes,
    - promotion from within,
    - a management style promoting participation, informality, visibility and accessibility,
    - insistence on high work standards.

While it was realized that no culture could be perfect in all these areas, a questionnaire containing open-ended questions was designed to test the respondents' perceptions concerning each of the characteristics listed above.

As a cluster sampling approach was used, the results were not valid in a strictly academic sense, but enough preliminary information was gathered to form a rough description of how the respondents viewed their working environment. For example, while it was the respondents' unanimous opinion that less than three years ago the work environment was 'friendly', 'trusting' and characterized by a family feeling, it was suggested that something had changed the ethos, or the central philosophy of the organization as set by the senior management team. With some exceptions, the respondents seemed to view senior personnel as aloof, uncaring and removed from the concerns of lower level personnel. This pronounced 'we/they attitude' could inhibit the effective operation of the organization, as many employees were beginning to feel alienated.

It was interesting to note that not all aspects of the culture were viewed as dysfunctional. At the lowest level of abstraction, the sytems area (work assignments, relationship with immediate supervisor etc., see Figure 10:1) perceptions generally were positive. Pay and benefits were seen as adequate and sexual discrimination was not an issue. Similarly, at the worker level, there was intense social interaction during work hours, suggesting the existence of an underlying homogeneity and commonality of interest. The problem, then, appeared to be that the top was out of touch with the bottom of the organization.

A training programme

The trainer's role in this instance was to act as a consultant. In practical terms, attending to corporate culture means starting at the top and working down through the organization so that the general ethos or philosophy of the work group is changed. As this 'attitude' toward the organizations' major activities is, in large measure, set by senior management, the consultant in this case made the following recommendations:

1   Senior management must be made visible. The Director and each of the Vice-Directors should spend at least one hour daily wandering about, chatting with employees in the lower echelons of the organization,
2   An intensive study must be made of the methods by which the various organizational levels communicate. Communication should be more intense and it must be more personal,
3   Although the process will take time, rites, rituals and rewards must be 'worked into the culture'.

The main training 'need' that surfaced from this analysis or profile, then, was to train senior management in the acquisition of a more open, people-oriented management style. Thus, the focus of training activity changed (for a time) from productivity and service issues at the bottom of the organization, to the top, where the existence of divergent cultural entities was not even suspected.

In this case, the 'training activity' would consist of developing a strategy (with the organization's Director) for changing the primarily authoritarian management philosophy, and then administering a series of non-threatening formal and informal sessions to 'train' senior management personnel in the art of organizational metamorphosis. This process would be supported by informal motivational sessions conducted privately by the Director culminating with the formal appraisal interview. It is suggested that this procedure will take from three to eight years, depending upon the size and complexity of the organization.

Cultural activities – their effect on the training function

At the second level of abstraction, the activities level (Figure 10.1), the trainer can focus on more traditional goals. For example, who would send a supervisor on a human relations course and then return that same individual to an authoritarian work environment where 'Theory X' is the dominant management style? Who would train in job description writing, in an organization where job descriptions are traditionally four years out of date and supervisors are not evaluated on their records-keeping abilities? Who would send junior managers to a communications course when the primary method of communication in their home organization is top-down with little room for feedback? Many senior and middle managers throughout North America and Europe will have to raise their hands in answer to these questions.

Support and maintenance systems in training

What then, should be done to integrate these activities into a cultural reality, to keep the training from becoming a 'cultural island', divorced from the mainland culture of the organization? (Figure 10:2). The answer goes beyond the traditional and necessary activity of training needs assessment to a study of support and maintenance systems. For until these two vital elements are in place, training should not proceed.

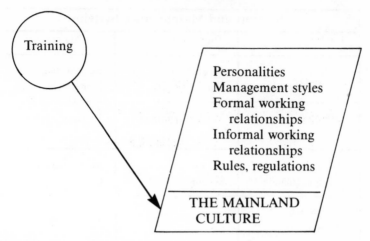

Figure 10:2   Training and the cultural island

Note: Reproduced with permission from the Institute of Training and Development.

A needs assessment in a health service organization by an outside consulting firm, for example, elicited the following concerns:

1   Budget planning,
2   Writing job descriptions,
3   Understanding job evaluation,
4   Line-staff relationships,
5   The selection process,
6   Orientation,
7   Performance management,
8   Stress management,
9   Conducting meetings,
10 Minute taking, and
11 Labour relations.

While it would not be difficult to design training modules for any of these topics, further investigation into the support and maintenance systems necessary to ensure training success (Figure 10:3), indicated that some would best be omitted, and others required further support.

Support and Maintenance Systems		
The Need	The Support	The Maintenance
1. Budget Planning	Budget planning and Control System	Regular Budget Planning Meetings
2. Writing Job Descriptions	Standard Format	Updating System
3. Understanding Job Evaluation	Job Evaluation System	Job Evaluation Committee
4. Line-staff Relationships		
5. The Selection Process	Policies & Controls re: Authority to Hire	
6. Orientation	Orientation Pro-gramme Developed	Check List for Follow up Session
7. Performance Management	Policy re: Perform-ance Mgmt. Problems	Employee files
8. Stress Management		
9. Conducting Meetings	Policy re: Authority to Call Meetings	
10. Minute Taking	Distribution System	File System
11. Labour Relations	Policy & System re: Grievance Processing	

Figure 10:3

Note: Reproduced with permission from the Institute of Training and Development.

The 'budget planning' process, for example, lacked a formal planning and central system which would require regularly-scheduled meetings between the management and the supervisory groups. While this procedure was not difficult to institute, it was suggested that job evaluation (setting pay to a job description) be omitted, as the organization was in the throes of negotiating a labour agreement and a common job description format did not as yet exist. Nor could orientation be taught immediately. Management wanted more study into what new employees really needed to know. The result of this support and maintenance analysis was to delay the training programme by several weeks. But when training did commence, it was with the assurance that learning would be directly related to what the trainees needed to know and that knowledge gained during the formal course work could be applied in the work environment. The provision of support and maintenance systems, then, brought the training from the 'cultural island' on to the mainland.

At this point it should be stressed that not all topics require support or maintenance. The request for more information concerning the Employment Standards Act could easily be met by obtaining copies of the Act and conducting a lecture/discussion while relating the salient points to current and possible organizational problems. A similar technique, fortified by the use of case studies, was found to be appropriate when presenting concepts such as motivation or informal groups. Even though the provision of support and maintenance systems is not a universal prerequisite for training, the process of analysing the state of one's own organization at the secondary or 'activities' level may be as valuable as the training itself, for the installation of support and maintenance functions that integrate training into the dominant culture, can result in a more effective operation.

Systems: The Bottom Line in Training Design

Cultural baggage

Much of the training in an organization takes place at the basic, or systems level, for it is here that the 'how to' function often takes place. It must be remembered, however, that the trainer deals with people, and people come complete with cultural baggage. Leonard

Nadler, in his superb book *Designing Training Programs*, tells the story of the 'Platform People'. In a certain bank in New York City, customers were using very few of the 35 services being offered to them. Nadler was asked to design a training programme for employees who normally sat at desks away from the tellers' cages – the Platform People. The idea was, that these individuals would leave their desks, meet customers, and sell the Bank's financial packages.

Unfortunately for the bank, this simple concept ran foul of cultural reality. It appears that a platform job was regarded as a promotion, a 'step up' in the world of banking. The desk itself was a symbol of long service and success and the Platform People 'had no intention of getting out from behind their desks'.

Accordingly, Nadler suggested that management either dismiss or transfer the Platform People and replace them with others not imbued with dysfunctional cultural values. His advice was ignored:

> ... and a contract was given to somebody else to design the training program. Within six months the vice-president for marketing was fired and a different person was hired. Jointly, with this action, new people were recruited and selected for the new job category. Some of the Platform people were retained for those activities which still needed to be done behind the desks. The new people hired knew that their main job performance was outside the bank, visiting customers, and selling bank services at the customers' place of business.

In other words, until the culture was changed (in this case destroyed) training would be ineffective in bringing about the massive changes required. As not every organization can adopt such expensive and Draconian measures, it is wise to take cultural attributes into account when designing a training programme, rather than wait until evaluation produces negative results.

The trainer/trainee dichotomy

Another aspect of culture that can affect training delivery systems is the trainer/trainee dichotomy. Too often, the trainer lives in a different cultural world from the trainees. Social class and community standing might be quite different, as well as age and educational achievement. With these differences come different value systems. For example, a book or a blueprint that is regarded with respect and valued as a 'good' thing in itself by a middle-class instructor, may be seen as a threatening object of suspicion and even punishment by working-class trainees. If books are not regarded as objects of value, time spent reading them or using them will not be valued. Therefore, trainees may be labelled as lazy or uninterested, when in fact, the wrong medium – one that has been rejected by the trainees' culture – is being used in the training process. Indeed, the mere sight of the traditional training room can trigger negative reaction and fear in some cultural groups.

Unless the trainer understands the cultural ramifications of his/her work, disrespect for the students is inevitable. The following, only slightly racist, joke has been told by staff (who are overwhelmingly of Anglo-Saxon origin) in a large training institution with a predominantly ethnic clientele:

Question: What do XYZ Institution and the Bata Shoe Company
              have in common?
Answer: They both have 5000 Italian Loafers.

This sort of we/they attitude will inevitably create tensions. When trainers lose respect for their trainees, the entire teaching/learning interface is negatively affected.

Introducing new technology – the challenge to training

Culture too, affects the introduction of new technology at a very basic or systems level, for cultural assumptions regulate employee receptivity to change. Is the workplace seen as a 'good' place in which to work? Does management treat employees fairly? 'The real power of culture . . . [may lie] in the area of assumptions – the way employees think about the organization' (Burdett, 1985). The trainer who works in a culture in which change is regarded as a constant rather than a threat, will not find the introduction of new concepts to be an onerous task. Conversely, if it is assumed that management has an uncaring, egocentric attitude toward 'rank and file' employees, cultural barriers will be thrown up to resist even the slightest change.

The trainer, then, may unwittingly find him/herself on the

receiving end of activities that are designed to block impending change. If an organization is to flourish, however, a constant influx of technical innovations must be accepted and utilized by both management and labour. This ability to introduce technological change can be a critical factor in the success or decline of individual business organizations and even entire industries. 'Indeed, how technology is introduced is increasingly seen as the key to ... workers' acceptance of it, which ultimately determines how much their productivity improves' (Financial Post, 1983).

Some years ago, as a junior systems analyst, I was responsible for training schedulers in the use of a computerized parts control system for a well known small appliance manufacturer. Several months after the system was 'on stream', it was found that considerable time still was being spent updating clandestine Kardex systems – kept hidden in desk drawers. While one might describe this incident as a reaction to fear of the unknown (computers for example, were not widely used at that time) recent evidence suggests that present-day workers and management are no better equipped than their predecessors for the inevitable onslaught of new technology.

Most authors, however, while admitting that resistance to change is extremely commonplace, indicate that often there are good reasons for intransigence. Individuals don't always resist change, they sometimes welcome it. 'What people do resist is change that threatens them or appears to threaten them because it has been sprung too suddenly, or it is too big an effort for them to grasp'. Some of the other difficulties that must be overcome include feelings of inadequacy and a fear by employees that they will be unable to cope with the training involved (Kleinscheid, 1980).

Part of the answer to this fear of the unknown, is in the use of a psychological technique that one might call 'success flagging', in which the instructor informs the students about the success of others who have gone before and/or suggests ways in which the trainees' jobs will be made easier, more profitable or whatever. In some cases, success flagging can be a simple statement: 'Not to worry Jane, I've taken many people through this process. I know you'll do all right.' Sometimes, time taken to complete a tour of a facility in which the new technology is operational can solve the problem. 'Borrowing' an employee who is familiar with the new technology – someone with the same cultural background and speech characteristics – from another employer or department can have beneficial results. The trainer must be innovative in designing methods to show employees that success is possible and that the new technology is used by other mere mortals like the present group of trainees.

Another major reason for resisting technological change is that the difference between old and new is too big to grasp. Frequently, time and financial constraints necessitate an intensive immersion into the new ways. These 'crash courses' can be more threatening than the new technology itself. In many cases it might be wiser to take a more deliberate approach, both as to time and teaching technique.

The title of a British Navy training film seen over 20 years ago, has long been relegated to the mists of memory, yet the scene in which the instrucor enters the classroom with an eight-by-four foot, fully detailed, schematic diagram of a jet engine, remains vivid. Of course, the trainees (actors all, I'm sure) were horrified at the thought of absorbing that amount of new information. The next sequence showed the same instructor and the same classroom, but this time the diagram was covered by pieces of taped-on paper, so that only a small section of the schematic showed. Predictably, the material was received in a more positive fashion.

Although this film illustrated an extreme case, the rate at which information can be acquired depends strongly upon culture. The trainer must take care to design learning experiences that 'match' the rate at which the trainees 'feel' they can absorb new data.

All efforts aimed at reassuring trainees will come to naught of course, if the instructors' actions are not compatible with the organization's overall cultural values. The process, then, has come full circle, in that while the trainer can create learning sytems that are culturally sound, the ability to introduce new technology depends, in large measure, upon how successful he/she has been in helping to develop management philosophies and cultural activities that support the change process by creating a climate of trust between management and other employees.

Orientation and the psychological contract

A final aspect of systems-level culture that must be addressed is the process of orientation. Much of what is done in industry is either superficial or of brief duration, when the employer should be taking the opportunity to socialize the new recruit into 'correct' cultural attitudes.

Pascale (1984) has outlined a seven-step orientation process:

1   An extremely lengthy and detailed selection process is designed to make sure the applicant will fit into the corporation's work environment or culture.
2   The employer makes the new employee do menial jobs that break down self esteem and cause him/her to question past beliefs and ways of thinking. This is done by giving the recruit more work than he/she can possibly complete so that outside social contacts are reduced to a minimum. By pushing the new employee to his/her physical and mental limits, 'vulnerability' is induced, making the recruit more susceptible to new cultural norms.
3   The 'newly humble recruits' are then sent to learn one of the firm's main businesses from the ground up. As the new recruit has been taught to think solely in terms dictated by the company's culture, this carefully supervised work experience solidifies these values and ensures that everyone works his/her way up from the same starting point.
4   At each step up the corporate ladder, the employer rewards the employee according to operating results.
5   The employer focuses continually on those values thought important to the firm's image and success – e.g. guaranteed service, the 'family feeling' – in order to give the employee some higher good than just serving a market. Goals might include 'serving mankind' or 'helping people learn and grow'.
6   The company reinforces its cultural values by consistently telling stories that support and reinforce acceptable conduct and methods of operation.
7   Consistent role models are supplied, so that the new recruit has an example to copy, further cementing 'correct' behaviour, attitudes and beliefs.

Where does the trainer 'fit' into this model? First, traditional orientation programmes must be redesigned so they act as entry portals into a new world – the trainer's corporation or public sector organization. This redesigning refocuses orientation activity from the short-term to a longer-term outlook lasting for perhaps, two years. During this time, the trainer acts as a consultant to management in the design and implementation of individual socialization and career development programmes.

These activities require skills different from those normally found in a training department. Here, the trainer becomes the advisor and confidant to the upper reaches of management, helping to chart the careers of future corporate leaders. Indeed, there seems to be little reason why this process cannot, in modified form, be used with employees at all levels. The three-tiered model of culture now has come full circle, in that the trainer may be working at all three levels of abstraction during the orientation process.

In the event that orientation programmes appear to be a one-sided, top-down indoctrination into the corporate lifestyle, it should be stressed that orientation must lead to a psychological contract – and *all* contracts are two sided. A psychological contract is the tacit understanding one reaches with a supervisor as to how the job should be done (Figure 10:4). This concept is particularly important in situations where trainees are likely to be transferred at frequent intervals.

Even though individuals have control over their decision to join a company, the criteria they use in making this decision often affect their future level of participation or effort. Indeed, while most individuals will make enquiries about items such as benefits and pay, few ask about the specific nature of the job or about future opportunity for personal development and growth – and even when they do ask, the response is likely to be perfunctory at best. Thus, they join with scant knowledge about what lies ahead. Should on-the-job reality not match initial expectations; should the work not fulfill needs for individual initiative, responsibility and challenge, the result can be frustration, poor or uneven performance and eventually, termination.

Given the likelihood, then, that the new employee will, at least to some extent, bring false conceptions and expectations to the job, it is vital that supervisors be trained in the management of

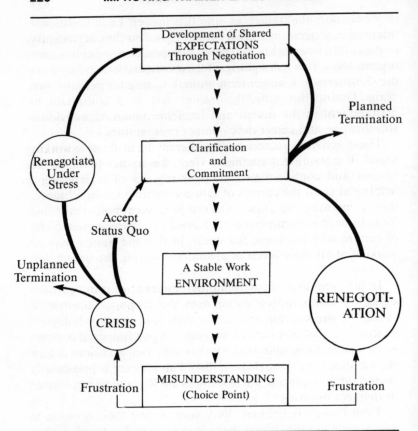

Figure 10:4 Management of the psychological contract

Note: Reproduced with permission from the Canadian Institute of Management. Adapted from Sherwood and Glidewell as quoted in Kolb et al. (1979).

psychological contracts. As indicated in Figure 10.4, 'the first stage in any relationship between two individuals and/or an individual and an organization, is characterized by a sharing of information and a negotiating of expectations.' Even in the unlikely event that expectations are fully and honestly shared, occasional misunderstanding will occur thus upsetting previously-agreed-upon-roles, rules and/or work relationships. The result of this upset is frustration, uncertainty, anxiety and/or resentment. Unfortunately, there is also a 'natural tendency' for managers, who are often preoccupied with production and other matters, to ignore the 'early warning signs . . . which signal a potentially disruptive situation' (Kolb et al, 1979).

Supervisors who take the time to acknowledge and to diffuse these misunderstandings are renegotiating (Figure 10:4) the original psychological contract in search of a new stable working environment. Those managers who choose to ignore, or are unaware that frustrations have developed, are choosing a different path, one that may lead to unplanned termination, or at best, a grudging acceptance of the new status quo within the organization. Indeed, forced acceptance of management's new norms can lead to the most insidious (and costly) type of termination – psychological termination in the form of apathy.

Aside from being aware that a psychological contract exists or does not exist, in practical terms, how can managers be trained to ensure its successful negotiation and inevitable renegotiation? The first step is to stress the importance of the key personnel documents – the job description, policy manuals and procedure specifications as it is in these sources that many on-the-job expectations are outlined. The next step is to train managers to help the employee set challenging, but achievable goals. Finally, honest and at first, frequent feedback should be stressed. It must be remembered that inexperienced employees need to be reassured more often than their more experienced counterparts. Those who have recently left school, for example, are accustomed to constant and immediate feedback – a grade or mark. They carry this expectation with them into the workforce. They are often shocked when their first manager seemingly is unconcerned with their day-to-day problems and anxieties.

The psychological contract, then, also includes the new employee's expectations of the organization and how these expectations can be met. The key variable in this process is expectation. It has long been known that if a teacher's expectations of students' classroom performance are low, performance will indeed be low; should instructor expectations be high, a higher level of learning will result. This concept applies as well to other social situations and to the work world, in that 'high expectations' on the part of the company can produce increased individual contribution, and great contributions will likewise raise expectations. Faced with this realization, the trainer's job is to make sure that managers have the social skills to prepare and to execute viable psychological contracts, not only at the entry levels, but at all stages in the career progression, be it transfer, promotion or the acceptance of a new position.

Managers ignore the concept of psychological contracts at their peril, for not only does an employee make a decision to join a given organization he/she also must make a decision to participate. It is in the level of this participation that most problems occur and where the trainer is most likely to become involved. But training activity directed at the poor performance may be addressing a symptom, when the real problem is a broken (and unmended) psychological contract.

CROSS-CULTURAL TRAINING ACTIVITY

The three-stage model now must be left behind to discuss an ever-growing area of training endeavour – cross-cultural training. The need to orient those who will be working abroad seems obvious, yet many companies involved in overseas endeavours do not provide in-depth preparation in the cultural aspects of the foreign experience. Even an innocuous posting or visit from say, Britain to Canada, can be fraught with embarrassment for the female company representative who innocently asks her Canadian host if he will 'knock me up in the morning'. The Britisher's request for a wakeup call is, in fact, a slang term for sexual intercourse.

How much more vital then, is it to orient employees who will work in Africa or the Far East. A recent trip to China to teach at a management college, for example, was preceded by three rigorous orientation sessions lasting a total of seven full days. We were taught mundane details such as never to blow one's nose at the table, how to wash and peel fruit, how to serve one's guest at a banquet and a host of other seeming trivia, yet without such detailed preparation, the trip might have been a disaster.

Often the trainer will not have visited the far-off climes to which company personnel will be sent. There may be no choice then, but to rely on others. When hiring so called 'experts' to orient one's staff, be cautious. Choose, not one, but a variety of individuals, including at least one medical expert. Past practice has shown that people interpret a foreign experience in terms of their own expectations and background: hence the trainer may get conflicting opinions and advice. In addition, be sure that the 'expert's' experience is of sufficiently long duration and recent enough to be relevant. A visit to a foreign country is quite different from living there for an extended period.

Not only must those who go to a foreign posting be trained, but those who administer the project at home also must be oriented. They should be reminded that the overseas manager or employee will live in a different culture and that business might not be conducted with the usual Western-style dispatch. In addition, they should be prepared for subtle (and sometimes not so subtle) changes in their employees' personality as the project progresses. The amount of personality change seems to depend upon whether or not the spouse and/or family accompany the employee. Despite the extra cost and obvious headaches, it is suggested strongly that family be included, as then the employee brings some of his/her culture along.

GUIDELINES FOR THE TRAINER

Whether at home or abroad, the trainer who is not fully conscious of the cultural milieu in which he/she works is doing only a partial job. It must be remembered that the training experience is itself a cultural phenomenon that must be inserted into an ever changing, always different, and sometimes resistant work environment, in such a way as to become an intrinsic part of the organization's overall cultural mosaic.

From the trainer's viewpoint, the development of a cultural profile appears to be a useful tool for influencing top management, for it is in the creation of a corporate philosophy that the organizations's cultural direction is determined. The key, then, is to adopt a consultant's role, advising senior management in the art of cultural development and manipulation.

After gaining an understanding of the culture in which he/she operates, the next task is to ensure that all training activity 'fits' the organization's cultural reality through careful application of support and maintenance systems. The trainer has a very personal stake in this process, as failure to provide adequate support and maintenance will severely limit programme effectiveness.

Finally, the trainer must know himself. An understanding of one's own 'cultural baggage' is critical if one is to deal effectively with others, who have different backgrounds. Constant awareness of the trainer/trainee dichotomy is the first step in developing a climate of mutual respect.

THE TRAINER'S CHECKLIST

1 Do I understand how the 'culture' of my organization works and how I fit into it?

2 What part or role does my department play?

3 Is the training activity extending far enough upward into the organization to exert an influence on basic managerial philosophy and style? If not, how can I begin to develop more influence?

4 Do I insist that credible support and maintenance systems be in place *before* I begin training?

5 Do I have enough influence to ensure the continued existence of maintenance systems?

6 Do I understand how the culture of my organization affects the willingness of trainees to learn and to accept new technology?

7 Do I understand and respect the cultural background of the trainees – who are my clients?

8 Am I able to design learning activities with the trainees' culture in mind?

9 Can I understand the trainees' viewpoint when new technology is introduced? Do I take steps to alleviate the fear that surrounds technological change?

10 Am I able to communicate the trainees' feelings to all levels of management? Do I try to do so!?

11 Is my department involved in orientation beyond the initial introduction to company norms? Does the orientation programme help to chart career progress, over an extended time period?

12 Does the training department help managers in the development of their psychological contracts?

13 Am I prepared to offer sound advice to those who are sent to foreign postings? Do I understand how vital this activity is?

14 Do I include both those who are going abroad and those who administer projects at home, in my orientation?

15 Do I search constantly for avenues to influence the culture of my organization?

REFERENCES/FURTHER READING

Burdett, J., 'Building A Values Driven Culture', *The Human Resource*, 1985, Oct/Nov. p. 21.

Campbell, A., 'Knowing "culture" of a firm is vital', *The Globe and Mail*, 1984, (Monday June 25) p. B3.

Drake, M.A., (1984) 'Information and Corporate Cultures', *Special Libraries*, 1984, (Oct.) p. 263.

Field, L.M., and Davies, A., 'Corporate Culture and Corporate Success', *The Canadian Manager*, 1984, (June), p.5.

The Financial Post, 'Companies' Workers Voice Concerns about VDTs', 1983, (Nov. 5), p. 51.

Hagedorn, H.J., 'Everybody into the Pool', *Across the Board*, 1984, (Oct.) p.26.

Kleinscheid, W.A., 'Change and the People Factor: A Matter of Trust, Not Technique', *Administrative Management*, 1980, vol. 41, May, p. 28.

Kolb, D.A., et al. *Organizational Psychology: An Experimental Approach* (3rd ed.), Prentice-Hall, Englewood Cliffs, New Jersey, 1979.

Nadler, L., *Designing Training Programs*, Addison-Wesley, Don Mills, 1982 p. 31.

Pascale, R., 'Fitting New Employees into the Corporate Culture', *Fortune*, 1984, May 28, pp. 28–34++.

Schwind, H.F., 'The State of the Art in Cross-Cultural Management Training', *International HRD Annual*, 1985, (vol. 1) Feb. p. 7.

Ulrich, W.L., 'HRM and Culture: History, Ritual and Myth', *Human Resources Management*, (1984) (Summer), p. 118.

Wright, P., 'Strategic Planning and Human Resources Development: The Vital Link', *Training and Development Journal*, 1983 Jan. pp. 16–17.

11 The Pursuit of Effectiveness

Roger Bennett

This book has been about improving trainer effectiveness. It has looked at the meaning of effectiveness, the changing context in which trainers have to operate, the factors influencing effectiveness, how to develop an effective role, how to operate effectively in particular roles, how the training function can operate effectively, the careers of trainers, and at the cultural reality of the trainer's world. The authors have provided insights into and guidance on various aspects of trainer effectiveness. The assumption has been that you, the reader, are pursuing effectiveness.

Although we can all talk about and practice effective behaviour in our various fields of endeavour, in many respects the pursuit of effectiveness in training is still a rather vague and elusive concept. We hope we have made it less vague and elusive. It is there to be obtained should we wish for it.

We now have some useful research-based indicators of training effectiveness. Some of these have been shared with you in previous chapters. In this final chapter we want to add to this by addressing two questions:

1   What makes for an effective training function?
2   What skills are required to survive and to continue to be effective as a trainer?

TRAINING FOR ORGANIZATIONAL EFFECTIVENESS

There is little doubt that the effective training function is one that continually strives to help the organization improve its effectiveness. The message has been repeated in several chapters – to be effective, the training function must get close to the 'heart' of the organization's business. It must be part of that business, not just reflecting it but actively striving to make that business a success. It must know the needs, talk the same language, and work to the same objectives.

We know from studies of organizational effectiveness how important training is. The Peters and Waterman study of US companies noted that 'there were enough signs of training intensity to state that training was highly related to organizational excellence...'. In the UK, Goldsmith and Clutterbuck noted the 'stress on training, both as a tool to increase efficiency and as a means of instilling the company's values into all employees', as a feature of successful companies. So the pursuit of effectiveness in training is, and must be, two-fold: it must improve the quality and excellence of the training activities, and it must improve the contribution it makes to the organization's success. The former does not necessarily lead to the latter. It can, however, if it pursues the same objectives – the organization's objectives.

But what makes for effective training? To answer this, we shall draw on two sources. In his *Handbook of Training Management,* Robinson lists the following factors:

- top management support and commitment, preferably direct involvement;
- the encouragement of team work, i.e. work achievement by co-operative effort towards defined goals;
- high standards of professionalism – a sound knowledge of training principles and methods and an intimate knowledge of the organisation and how it works – a reputation established by a good track record in identifying and satisfying needs;
- skill in recognising the necessity for change and being able to handle it efficiently;
- adaptability in responding to varying individual and group characteristics;

- evaluation procedures which enable training activities to be monitored and if necessary modified, and
- recognition that training should be cost effective.
  (pp. 207 and 208)

Many of these factors echo messages coming through from a number of the previous chapters.

The second source is the collated experience of training consultants working with hundreds of successful companies of all sizes. The consultants work for Zenger-Miller Inc. in the United States. In a superb paper on training for organizational excellence, Zenger identifies ten factors for success. These can be described as follows:

1   A clear vision of the goal and mission of training.

> 'The best training functions are absolutely clear about the distinction between traditional education and the role of industrial training. They see their primary function as giving people practical skills that they can immediately use on the job. Their major emphasis is not education. They teach theory and information where it is relevant to the demands of the job.
>
> The training function's focus is on behaviour change that occurs on the job. There is less concern about 'awareness' and 'insights' and more concern with action plans.'
>
> 'Effective training organizations see their roles as helping to define, clarify and convey the values and culture of the organization. They see training as a prime vehicle for executives to transmit their philosophy and values. Underlying this clear vision of the goal and mission of training is a deep and unswerving conviction that training really makes a difference in the daily performance of the organization.'

2   Tightly linked to the organization's objectives.

> 'The effective training functions keep riveted to their organization's goals. They are constantly aware of the mission, goals and the genuine needs of the organization. They stay aware of these in a variety of ways, sometimes

informal, and sometimes highly structured and formal. But, they always channel training to the genuine needs of the organization.

Their goal is to contribute to organization excellence, by helping the organization with its immediate goals or training needs. They develop a master plan of training that interlocks with the corporation master plan and tactical objectives. They are systems oriented. They see the big picture.'

3   Line management commitment and involvement.

'While all organizations talk of management involvement and support, we suspect that many training functions really receive *permission* instead of true support. They are given permission to spend money and take people's time, but real ownership of line management is often lacking.

The top training functions, by contrast, have generated an enthusiastic involvement in line managers. Line managers participate in defining training objectives all the way to the actual delivery of the training.'

4   Excellent management practice within the training function.

'The training function in excellent companies practices what it teaches. The budgets are submitted on time. The secretaries answer the telephone efficiently and court-eously. Members are willing to take risks and experiment. They accept responsibility and make themselves accoun-table for a return on the investment the organization makes in training. They are participative in their own management, but hold people accountable for high level performance. They are technically competent and knowled-geable about training content, methods and manage-ment.'

5   Emphasis on practicality.

'During the last decade, we have witnessed a profound shift away from esoteric, theoretical, complex training. We see a strong movement towards the more practical, concrete, "what do I do on Monday morning" training.

This is especially true of the *content* of training. Rather than lecturing employees on the importance of being customer oriented, the best training functions emphasize simple things like, "answer the phone after the second ring", "call the customer by name", or "return telephone calls promptly". Instead of lectures to supervisors on Maslow's need hierarchy, we see the best training functions having supervisors rehearse the skills of listening, asking questions, clarifying goals, and coaching.'

'Top training functions move toward practical teaching *methods* to teach their practical content.'

'Top training functions emphasize *relevancy.*'

'The top training functions are highly resourceful. They know how to get the best job done, in the quickest time.

The best training functions also know that training is not always the right answer.'

6   They use multiple resources to assist them.

'We observe that the most effective training functions do not attempt to design or conduct all of the training themselves. Instead, they see themselves as orchestrators, who marshal all available resources to provide the needed training activity. They are not jealous of line managers' conducting training, outside consultants with specialized skills, or outside organizations which design instructional systems. They see themselves as the group responsible for making training occur, but not the ones who personally must do it all.'

7   Consistent delivery.

'If a service is to be satisfactory in the long run, it must be of consistently high quality. The same training course often receives rave reviews and strong criticism when different people conduct it. We have observed that the excellent training functions find ways to make training consistent. One approach is frequent monitoring of trainers to ensure uniformity and quality of delivery and content. Another is to emphasize the quality of materials and learning designs. By placing more emphasis on learning design, materials, and technology, in addition to the trainer, greater consistency may be obtained.'

8   Sense of urgency.

'The effective training functions bring a high energy and intensity to the task. They are less reflective, introspective, and philosophical. They are deeply action oriented and have a desire to get on with things, quickly. They model exactly the same behaviour they seek from all managers.'

9   Achieve critical mass.

'Many training departments talk of numbers of training days, and measure their performance on training hours or days conducted. True, we observe that the more effective organizations are doing extensive amounts of training. It reflects their commitment. But, they emphasize a handful of core courses that impact a large percentage of the target population.'

10   Evaluation of results.

'While we do not see ALL of the excellent training functions spending time and money on quantitative evaluation of training results, we consistently see a deep commitment to find practical ways to determine if training is really paying off. They evaluate training using the measures that seem most relevant to the management of their own organization. Meaningful evaluation is always in the eye of the beholder.'

We have been able to use only selective quotes from Zenger's paper. He goes much deeper into explanation and provides many good examples and commentary. What we hope to have achieved is to convey a clear message about what makes for effective training. The message is not dissimilar from that of Robinson nor is it in conflict with the messages coming through this book as a whole. That message can be simply stated:

● *get to know who your customers are, find out what their needs are, and make sure you satisfy these needs efficiently.*

TRAINING EFFECTIVENESS CHECKLIST

In pursuing effectiveness, you might do well to assess your training function against the factors derived from the two above sources. How well does the training function compare against them? Rate each factor by placing a 4,3,2,1 or 0 on each line:

we achieve this factor

completely	-	4
to a good extent	-	3
partly	-	2
very little	-	1
not at all	-	0

- clear view of goal and mission _____
- tight links with organization's objectives _____
- excellent management of training function _____
- emphasis on practicality _____
- use of multi-sources _____
- consistent delivery _____
- sense of urgency _____
- critical mass _____
- evaluation of results _____
- good team work _____
- high professionalism _____
- recognition of change _____
- adaptability in response _____
- cost effectiveness _____

Total score _____

If your total score approaches 60, you are doing well. If it is around 30, you can improve. If it is below 30, you have some essential development work to undertake.

INDIVIDUAL EFFECTIVENESS

The pursuit of training effectiveness is fruitless if individual trainers are not effective. A successful training department or group depends for that success on the contributions made by its members. Equally, a lone star performer will have little impact on the effectiveness of the wider group unless there are others who can be encouraged to pursue effectiveness – both 'overall' and 'interim' effectiveness. The pursuit of effectiveness is thus a two-way process. We have summarized the main factors that help the training function to become effective. Now we turn our attention to the individual.

Chapter 2 discussed the main factors that influence trainer effectiveness. It is worth pulling these together and adding to some of the key skills needed to survive as a trainer and to continue to be effective.

The study carried out by Bennett and Leduchowicz revealed eight main factors that contributed to individual effectiveness.

1   *Trainer skills.* The effective trainer possesses skills in two main areas; dealing with people, and dealing with training. The 'people skills' include being able to gain access to people in the organization, to get co-operation from them, and to work well with senior staff. Many of these skills are crucial in securing commitment to training and shaping training to the needs of the organization. They are political in part, and influence strongly overall effectiveness. The 'training' skills are those we would normally associate with doing a competent job on a training programme or workshop. The main ones were knowledge and experience of the subject matter or area of training (including the organization and its procedures/products): knowledge and experience of training design, methods and techniques: analytical ability (especially in analysing problems and learning difficulties): being creative in the development and design of training events; and being competent at administration and management in general.

2   *Personal characteristics.* The effective use of skills depends very much on the personal characteristics of the trainer. Two characteristics stand out from the rest: being sensitive and

responsive to the needs of those being trained, and being genuinely interested in the subject matter or area of training. These are things that are primarily about classroom-based training, and this raises an important issue. Is trainer effectiveness concerned only with 'instruction' or 'teaching'? It is not. The truly effective trainer possesses other important characteristics too – among them patience, humour, confidence, neat appearance, tolerance of ambiguity and credibility!

3   *Work behaviour or approach.* Trainers adopt different approaches or patterns of work behaviour, called 'trainer style'. For example, in one company, many trainers saw themselves as the focus of activity, were directive in approach, and used lecture/information giving approaches quite extensively. They were very 'trainer centred'. In another company, the trainers were more participative and open in their approach, and were led by the needs, requirements and interests of the trainees. These trainers were very 'trainee centred'. Other aspects of effective work behaviour included good pre-course preparation/research, evaluating training to improve performance, follow-up of trainees, good use of practical examples and adapting/changing instructional approach to suit the needs of trainers. Work behaviour is, in the main, associated with interim effectiveness.

4   *Perception of the job.* Trainers have different views or perceptions of their job/role ('role orientation'). Some see their work very much in terms of a traditional educational or professional model. Here someone else is responsible for identifying organizational needs, selecting those needs that can be tackled through training and working up a training objective. The trainer's role is to set up a suitable course or programme that can achieve the set training objective.

Other trainers see their job to be more concerned with finding out what the organization really needs to survive, change and develop. Such trainers use 'interventionist' strategies closely related to those that organization development (OD) practitioners adopt.

Some trainers also see their work to be about helping to

support current organization requirements. It is mainly a maintenance activity. They adopt fire-fighting approaches to training and aim to help maintain levels of performance.

Contrasted to this are trainers who see their main task as bringing about change in the systems, procedures or technologies of the organization. They try to anticipate the effects of changes in the environment and to prepare people for the subsequent organizational change. These perceptions suggested four main types of trainer – the 'caretaker', 'educator', 'evangelist', and 'innovator'.

5   *Nature of the job.* Trainers work at a variety of different jobs, i.e. they adopt different roles. It is clear that there is no one best role. But what do we mean by 'role'? It refers to the collection of behaviours, attitudes and values that are expected of the trainer. The research identified a wide range of roles. In essence, they cover such aspects as giving direction to the training effort, determining goals, preparing initiatives, implementing initiatives, evaluating outcomes, and developing resources.

6   *Organizational needs.* To survive, the trainer must meet or satisfy the needs of the organization for training. However, this must not be achieved at the expense of professional integrity. Sometimes, trainers may have to resign because they cannot reconcile their professional approach and ethics with the requirements of the company. For example, in one of our case studies, the senior training person could have easily given in to the company's need for professional, highly programmed courses. Instead, he saw a need for the company to change and developed his strategy accordingly, but it was a rough ride for a few years.

7   *Purpose of training.* What a trainer does and how well it is done are shaped by how clearly defined is the training purpose. Whether or not the trainer agrees with the purpose will affect the level of motivation to do the job. Thus, both clarity and nature of purpose are important – they tell the trainer what is expected and when it is to be achieved. In a sense, this is the

training equivalent of management by objectives. Without a purpose, there can be only a vague notion of what is to be done. This makes for difficulties in assessing effectiveness. We need to sort out our purposes into those that really are of great importance to the organization and are either critical to the jobs people do or are difficult to achieve; those that have some importance and are necessary to achieve but not critical to performance; and those that are of low importance and perhaps, easy to achieve.

8   *Type of organization.* Organizations are often characterized by their nature, their 'climate' or their 'culture'. This refers to the attitudes, feelings and state of interpersonal relations. This 'organizational culture' does influence trainer effectiveness, particularly how trainers go about their jobs as well as what they do.

Of considerable influence is the style and approach used by senior management, especially the managing director or chief executive. Trainers ought to be (and many are) seeking to influence positively the attitudes of senior managers and 'selling' the training message. They sometimes cannot escape being in the hot seat, feeling uncomfortable, but knowing they need to push on.

We found that these eight factors were important on their own in influencing trainer effectiveness. Together, they become almost explosive. They influence each other in a way that can produce very strong positive or negative influences. Our experience is that organizations must achieve the proper fit between these factors – a 'dynamic balance', for trainers to be effective. In some cases, the organization will have to change the training personnel to get the right fit. We have come across several cases where, because of rapid product technology and organizational changes, trainers can't cope or adapt. Although this is sad, it is a fact that has to be faced.

SURVIVING FOR TOMORROW

So far we have considered eight key factors that appear to be important in determining trainer effectiveness. However, the trainer has to survive to continue being effective. Clearly, the effective trainer has a greater chance of surviving than the ineffective trainer, but can this continue into the future? Our work with trainers around the world suggests that there are four key sets of skills that the trainer will need to survive for tomorrow.

1 *Technical skills.* These include skills in the area of training, the organization as a whole, the business of the organization and the environment. To survive, the trainer must be skilled at more than just the technology/methods of training. The surviving trainer will be able to carry out organizational analysis, business planning activities, and help managers assess the business environment. In essence, the skills of survival will include much more than training skills and will overlap the skills required by the business consultant and organization development practitioner.

2 *Personal skills.* We have already seen that personal skills or characteristics help effective trainers put into practice their other skills. This will be true in surviving for the future. Trainers will have to be skilled at communicating information, ideas, thoughts, plans etc., to others in the organization; to be skilled at generating enthusiasm for training policies; to be skilled at analysing managerial and business situations and translating those into training needs and support, and to be skilled at generating a high degree of acceptability with colleagues in the organization.

3 *Political skills.* These will operate in support of both technical and personal skills. In other words, whilst it will be important for survival to possess both technical and personal skills, it will not be sufficient. We have found that the trainers most likely to survive are those who have a good degree of visibility and credibility within the organization. That is they are seen to be around and to be doing a good job, they are able to link in with the appropriate power base in the organization (that is, they have identified who really makes the decisions and get close to those people), and they are able to persuade and influence what happens within the organization. Skills in each of these areas can be developed.

4   *Innovatory skills.* These both support and are supported by the
three skill areas just outlined. In order to survive and make a
successful contribution to the organization, trainers will be
helping to bring about change and perhaps even suggesting
change in areas that are appropriate to business survival and
regeneration. To do this trainers must be skilled in the
following areas: scanning the environment to see what is
happening and what new processes and products can be
brought into the company; generating ideas that can be
considered by managers as ways of helping to push ahead;
experimenting, or helping managers to experiment with new
approaches, ideas, processes and so on; and helping the
organization to learn, that is, making sure that what one
manager does successfully through innovation is shared with
the rest of the organization so that managers as a team learn
what is happening individually and on a small group basis in
the company.

These four skill areas are, we would suggest, the most
important that trainers will have to work at in the near future if
they are to survive. However, the most successful trainers, in terms
of surviving and continuing to make a positive contribution to the
profitability and general success of the organization, will be
visionaries. They will be able to take a long-term view of the
organization and the training activity and will be able to work
through with senior managers, various scenarios and possibilities
for the future. They will, in effect, be members in their own right of
the forward planning and corporate strategy setting process of the
organization.

The factors and skills described above can be used as the basis
of a checklist for assisting trainer effectiveness. A fairly full and
detailed checklist is presented in Appendix B. Work through the
checklist. When you have finished, ask yourself the following
questions:

1   in what areas am I already effective? and

2   in what areas am I not so effective?

The pursuit of effectiveness will be aided greatly if you can
build on your strong areas and do something about the weaker

ones. We hope this book will have provided you with some thoughts, insights and practical approaches for doing this.

Remember – your organization and its training needs will almost certainly be undergoing change. This may require you to change, also. What are currently your strong areas may not be so in the future. The pursuit of effectiveness requires you to change, to develop new areas of strength and to be flexible, adaptive and responsive.

REFERENCES/FURTHER READING

Sources on trainer and training effectiveness

Bennett, R. and Leduchowicz, T., 'What Makes for an Effective Trainer?', *Journal of European Industrial Training Monograph*, 1983, vol. 7, no. 2.

Robinson, K., *A Handbook of Training Management,* Kogan Page, London, 1985.

Zenger, J., 'Training for Organisational Excellence', *STADA Annual* (Singapore Training and Development Association), 1985.

Studies of successful organizations

Goldsmith, W., and Clutterbuck, D., *The Winning Streak,* Weidenfeld and Nicolson, London, 1984.

Peters, T., and Waterman, R., *In Search of Excellence,* Harper & Row, New York, 1982.

Appendix A. Developing Trainer Effectiveness – Two Model Programmes

Roger Bennett

Since 1980 I have been involved in numerous conference presentations, seminars and workshops, in the UK and overseas, on trainer effectiveness. Most of these have been based, in part, on research and development work carried out for the UK's Manpower Services Commission. A clear message has been derived from all these activities – namely, while research findings and conceptual frameworks about trainer effectiveness are important ingredients for getting trainers and training managers to think afresh about effectiveness, something more is called for. That 'something more' is the *active* involvement of participants in working through issues and developing action plans. Then, the plans must be put into operation and reviewed.

Not all activities go through to action and review. This depends on the objectives. If the aim is to stimulate thinking about effectiveness, a half or one day seminar will be appropriate. For action and review, a three to five day workshop with a follow-up day some months later will be necessary. Variations on these can, of course, be designed. The key is to decide in advance what you want participants to gain from the event. Events I have been involved with have been for academic/training institutions and public/private sector organizations. Each had different aims, and the events designed accordingly. You will have to decide your aims and the approach best suited to them. However, it may be helpful to outline just two of the approaches I have used, to act as thought provokers. The first is a one-day seminar used in various forms for educational and training purposes. The second is a four-day workshop, again used in slightly different forms, for developing company trainers.

ONE DAY SEMINAR

Aim: to provoke new thinking about the factors that influence trainer effectiveness and the different roles trainers can adopt.

Participants: new trainers, or experienced trainers, or training managers (a mix can be stimulating).

Group size: the smaller the better, but can be as high as 20 plus.

Facilities required: main seminar room for plenary inputs and reporting back, several discussion rooms, OHP, plenty of flip-charts.

Tutors: one is usually sufficient; two are very useful.

Outline programme:

9.00–10.30   Introductions plus expectations.   (30 mins)
Individually – participants think of an effective trainer and describe on paper, using key words or short phrases OR list five factors important in being effective.   (15 mins)
Small Groups – share lists, and agree common list of most important items.   (45 mins)

10.30–11.00   Coffee

11.00–12.30   Plenary – groups report, using prepared flip charts, and discuss; input from tutor on research findings/experience about effectiveness, with discussion.

12.30–2.00   Lunch

2.00–3.30   Individually – participants complete brief questionnaire on what they do in their job now.
      (15 mins)
Small groups (of 3) – participants share and discuss findings, and help each determine what areas of work should be changed to meet future requirements.
      (75 mins)

3.30–4.00   Tea

4.00–5.30   Plenary – individual reports (in brief) on key areas of change.
Input – the roles of the trainer and their relevance to different business/organizational requirements; helpful frameworks for thinking about the job; discussion and summary; issue of handouts, checklists, etc.

FOUR-DAY WORKSHOP WITH FOLLOW-UP

Aim: to develop and review more effective ways of training.

Participants: preferably, experienced trainers or training managers faced with a need to change or adopt new approaches.

Group size: twelve is ideal, but 18 can be handled.

Facilities required: main room for plenary session and up to six work rooms or work areas; OHP; plenty of flip charts; video recorder.

Tutors: at least two – if individual counselling is required, more may be needed.

Pre-workshop preparation by participants: some basic reading on trainer effectiveness; completion of pro-forma describing job, responsibilities, etc; completion of questionnaire for discussion purposes (if one is to be used in workshop); discussion of programme objectives, expectations and support with boss.

Outline programme:

Day 1
-   introductions, scene setting, agreement of objectives and expectations.
-   assessment of factors influencing trainer effectiveness (individual and small groups as per one day seminar).
-   written identification of key factors influencing *their* jobs, in small consultant groups of three, each member probing the others about the real nature of their jobs.

- individual production and presentation of statement of positive and negative factors influencing their jobs, with constructive discussion on each.

Day 2
- input on trainer effectiveness, with discussion.
- individual revision of statements, if necessary, plus choice of areas/factors they wish to do something about.
- consultant groups discuss, review and agree each set of action areas.
- presentation of action areas in plenary, with discussion.
- assessment of trainer roles currently adopted (via, e.g., questionnaire analysis discussed in small groups).
- input on trainer roles, and how trainers can influence others.

Day 3
- review of outcomes of day 2 and revision of action areas to incorporate roles and influences.
- development of action plans in consultant groups (most of the day will be needed for this); individual/group discussions with tutor.

Day 4
- finalization of action plans ready for presentation; presentation of individual action plans in plenary, using flip charts, OHP etc., and recorded on video. Summary and review. Agree follow-up.

N.B. Tutors will need to prepare briefs in advance for some of these activities and will require a detailed running order that they must be prepared to abandon – it is a guide only. The emphasis must be on flexibility and adaptability. Handouts, checklists and questionnaires must be available to help those participants who need to do a bit more 'thinking through'.

Follow-up day:

Agreed at the end of workshop, for some 3–6 months hence. Participants will reconvene, show their videos on individual basis, state what has been done and discuss further requirements.

Such a workshop will be found to be exhausting but fruitful by both tutors and participants.

This is, of course, just one possible pattern for the workshop, and one that seems to work very well. The general theme of analysis, review, consolidation, critique, re-statement and action is generally applicable. Different emphases will be required by different sets of participants. One workshop might require more analysis/input of sources of power and influence, another a greater understanding of roles and how they can be developed, yet another the development of specific skills. Pre-workshop interviews with intending participants, or the use of a pre-workshop questionnaire, will help spot these needs. However, the stress *must* be on flexibility within the workshop itself.

ACKNOWLEDGEMENTS

Many organizations have been involved in events similar to those described above, with myself as a co-partner in designing and running them. The experience gained by all has been well worth the effort. Thanks for this are due to the Civil Service Staff College, Manchester University, Slough College, the Singapore Government, MCE (Brussells), the Manpower Services Commission, Rothman's International (for a related programme for managers) and United Biscuits.

Appendix B. The Effective Trainer Checklist

The research and workshops on trainer effectiveness carried out by staff of the then Thames Valley Regional Management Centre at Slough and Oxford, on behalf of the Manpower Services Commission, identified a number of key areas that influence trainer effectiveness. This checklist summarizes what were found to be the more important factors in each area. The purpose of the checklist is to provide some food for thought: it is not a definitive listing. All items must be considered in the light of the trainer's own situation. In using this checklist, you are invited to ask the following questions:

- how does this apply to me?

- where do I stand in relation to each item?

- where should I be?

- what things might I change to improve my effectiveness?

- why should I change?

This checklist draws upon research sponsored by the Manpower Services Commission and on workshops, seminars and conferences conducted throughout the UK and overseas. Hundreds of trainers and managers contributed to the work on which it is based. Their contribution is warmly appreciated, as is the work of Tad Leduchowicz, of Slough College, who was Research Associate on the main project.

- how can I bring about the change?

- what help do I need to change?

- what other factors should I be considering?

There are no right or wrong answers. The process of asking and answering the questions will help clarify what you want or need to do to improve the contribution you can make to your organization.

TRAINER COMPETENCIES

These can be numerous, but our research suggests the following at least must be considered:

- ability to motivate learners and to hold their interest

- capacity to communicate and present information, and ideas, in a meaningful way

- good knowledge of the subject matter or area in which people are being trained

- ability to relate the training to the practical world of the trainees, using appropriate examples

- clarity of thought and in use of analytical and logical skills

- capacity to stand back and work strategically

- being able to control the learning group

- exercising appropriate social and leadership skills

- being able to manage the training situation.

There will be others you would wish to add, based on your own experience.

Please do so:

_____
_____
_____
_____

TRAINER CHARACTERISTICS

The range of characteristics is clearly very diverse – as diverse as the people who make up the training profession. However, the research indicates the following to be important contributions to effectiveness:

- being sensitive to the needs of the learners

- being prepared to listen to what learners have to say

- being approachable, responsive and sensitive, feeling the mood of the learners

- projecting enthusiasm, vitality, motivation, interest and dedication

- having confidence in and commitment to the approach adopted

- being patient and tolerant of the learners' problems and shortcomings

- being seen to be 'credible'.

Others you would wish to add:

_____
_____
_____
_____

TRAINER ROLE ORIENTATION

This refers to the way in which the trainer sees the role. Two key dimensions were established from the research, and imply four basic orientations. Which orientation do you have?

- an orientation to the maintenance needs of the organization, that is, to ensuring the continuance of the existing activities, products or services

- an orientation to bringing about change within the organization, that is, to ensure that training can respond to pressures for change from both outside and inside the organization to help it get geared up to meet new situations, objectives etc.

- an orientation to traditional methods of training, that is, methods and approaches adopting the educational or 'professional' model of training based largely on classroom-type techniques and curriculum design

- an orientation to methods of intervention, that is, a 'change agent' approach to training that involves greater participation in bringing about changes in systems, procedures or technologies and in changing peoples' attitudes and approaches to work.

Do you have others?

_____

_____

_____

_____

TRAINER STYLE

There exist considerable variations in the way in which trainers go about their jobs. We found that a number of dimensions could be used to characterize trainer style. Where do you fit on each of these dimensions?

1. Use trainer-centred   Use learner-centred
   training approaches   _____   training approaches

2. Use persuasion to get people involved in training

Use own authority or the authority of others to get people involved in training

———

3. Work in a detached way

Am pervasive in the organization

———

4. Adopts theory-centred approaches in training

Adopts problem or need centred approaches in training

———

5. Use interventionist strategies

Do not use interventionist strategies

———

6. Primary concern is for the need of the organization

Primary concern is for the needs of the individual

———

7. Respond to training needs as presented to you

Diagnose the nature of apparent training needs before responding

———

8. Structures training programmes highly

Adopts a more flexible approach to training programme structure

———

9. Use standard/tried training approaches

Experiments with training approaches

———

10. Tend to propose solution

Guide people through problem-solving

———

11. Work strategically, plans ahead and sets objectives

Responds to problems and needs as they arise

———

12. Takes steps to remain informed on subject matter and the organization

Do not take steps to remain informed on subject matter and the organization

———

13. Chooses specific areas   Am more concerned with
    for training initiatives   teaching principles
    _____

14. Obtains feedback to   Not concerned with
    improve training   obtaining feedback
    _____

15. Varies training   Tend to use the same
    approaches to suit   training approach
    learners   irrespective of type of
                                  learners
    _____

Are there other dimensions you would add?

_____
_____
_____
_____

TRAINER ROLES

There is clearly no one, all purpose trainer role. Trainers adopt a
variety of roles, some being merged within an overall role. Which
of the following roles do you perform?

- Training Policy Formulator

- Training Need Identifier and Diagnostician

- Generator of Ideas for Training Initiatives

- Formulator of Training Objectives

- Researcher and Curriculum Builder

- Materials Designer and Developer

- Training Administrator and Organizer

- Training Marketeer

- Direct Trainer/Instructor

- OD Agent, Catalyst, Facilitator

- Coach, Mentor

- Training Advisor, Consultant

- Agent of Learning Transfer to the Job

- Manager of Training Resources

- Trainer and Developer of Trainers

- Liaison Officer

- Assessor of Training Quality

- Evaluator of Training Contribution

What others would you add?

_____
_____
_____
_____

ORGANIZATION CULTURE

Trainers operate in rather different cultures according to the nature of the organization in which they work. Many things characterize organization culture. The following represent a few of the key ones:

- the extent to which the organization is managed in an autocratic or democratic manner

- the attitude of managers toward the training function

- the level of involvement of line managers in the training activity

- the degree of support for training, particularly at senior management level

- the philosophy of the organization concerning education, training and staff development

- the time span of senior management, that is, 'results today' or 'better performance in the future', or both

- the nature and use of power in the organization (e.g. personal power versus positional power)

- the nature and use of sanctions

- the form and nature of technology and the work to be performed.

Please add others of your own:

_____

_____

_____

_____

You will need to weigh up the kind of culture in which you operate and adopt a style appropriate to it – or seek to change it!

ORGANIZATIONAL NEEDS

It is difficult to be specific about these, since they are unique to the organization in question. However, you may wish to consider which of the following you are trying to satisfy:

- ensuring adequate supply of properly trained personnel

- keeping present job performance levels up to scratch

- developing skills, abilities and attitudes for future job performance requirements

- building greater job deployment flexibility

- coping with fast-changing technologies

- moving into new markets

- meeting statutory training requirements

- coping with reduced staffing levels and redundancy

- preparing staff for retirement.

You can no doubt add specific needs that your organization is trying to meet:

_____

_____

_____

_____

PURPOSE OF TRAINING

These are really for you to define, in the light of the organizational needs that have to be met. But think about the following:

- is training part of a general corporate strategy for improving organizational effectiveness?

- is training carried out because it has a long history of existence in the organization: we do it because we've always done it?

- is training too concerned with satisfying external requirements (e.g. of Government, of ITBs)?

Any others?

_____

_____

_____

_____

OVERALL EFFECTIVENESS

Finally, what do you feel are the outcomes of your work as a trainer. Are they:

- evidence of changed behaviour/performance of trainees?

- capacity of trainees to continue to apply learning to their work situations?

- greater willingness of trainees to find better ways of doing things?

- improvement in the cost effectiveness and efficiency of the organization?

- improved productivity?

- greater interest in training, e.g. as expressed in more post-training follow-up activities?

- measureable achievement of objectives?

Others:

_____
_____
_____
_____

SURVIVING AS A TRAINER

Trainers are increasingly under threat from economic pressures, the introduction of new technology and organization restructuring. To survive the threat and continue to make a positive contribution to the organization requires certain skills. These are listed below. What are you good/less good at? Which ones need developing? Who can help you develop them?

Technical

Skilled at:
- training methods and techniques
- analysing organizational behaviour/structures
- helping plan the business activities
- identifying environmental changes.

Personal

Skilled at:
- communicating ideas effectively
- analysing training/business needs clearly and logically
- generating enthusiasm for training
- building acceptance of your skills/ role as a trainer.

Political

Skilled at:
- being visible to others within the organization
- persuading others to support training
- influencing events and decisions in the organization
- identifying and getting close to the real sources of power in the organization.

Innovating

Skilled at:
- scanning the external environment for new ideas/new approaches that might be helpful to your organization
- generating new ideas for consideration by colleagues
- experimenting with new ideas/ approaches to demonstrate their usefulness in helping to meet business requirements

> - helping the organization to learn
> from the uses of new approaches
> and develop more effective ways
> of surviving and meeting the busi-
> ness challenge.

You might have others – list them here:

_____

_____

_____

_____

_____

Remember, the best means of survival is to make a direct contribution to the organization's business needs – to help it survive and grow. Check which activities you engage upon meet this requirement. For those that don't, can you afford to continue with them?

Let us repeat that this checklist is not an exhaustive set of factors – it is a 'starter for ten' aimed at getting you to think about yourself as a trainer. We hope it will help you focus on items that could benefit from greater attention. But please bear in mind one important conclusion from the research – there must be the right kind of fit or congruence between each area. The role you adopt must fit the organization culture, or its needs – even if it really means being a bit of an irritant. Also bear in mind that successful 'irritants' have a power base somewhere in the organization!

Annotated Reading List

Roger Bennett

The readings in this section have been selected to provide further opportunities for exploring some of the key issues and points raised in the text. They are not meant to be representative of the complete range of material available. Some go into considerable depth on the topic, others are more broadly based. The notes under each title will, we hope, give you a fair indication of what is covered and the depth gone into.

We are grateful to Trainer Support Services for allowing us to draw upon material developed for them by the Editor.

Abramson, R. and Halset, W., *Planning for Improved Enterprise Performance – A Guide for Managers and Consultants,* ILO, Geneva 1979.

Invaluable, practical approach to OD-based performance improvement. Three parts: (1) the PIP approach (what is OD and planning, model of the process, introduction to PIP workshops and instruments, details of workshop methodology, case study); (2) planning and managing action programmes (management and control, MBO, examples, evaluation and selecting programmes etc); and (3) applicability/impact of PIP. Appendices include the performance improvement instrument, team effectiveness rating forms, measures of organizational effectiveness, and a selected bibliography. Very good for trainers wanting to develop performance improvement consultancy/advisory programmes/skills.

Bennett, R. and Leduchowicz, T., 'What makes for an Effective Trainer?', *Journal of European Industrial Training Monograph*, MCB, Bradford, 1983, vol. 7 no. 2.

Describes findings of MSC-sponsored study. Sections cover: why bother looking at trainer effectiveness?; approach used; major findings; case example of effective trainer in modern industry; key aspects of trainer effectiveness; an approach to looking at trainer effectiveness.

Major findings cover: what kinds of people are trainers?; what kinds of organizations do they work for?; what do trainers do?; what problems/constraints do trainers encounter?; what criteria relate to trainer effectiveness; what constitutes trainer credibility?; how can trainers improve their contribution to the organization?; on what basis should trainers be selected? Framework of role types and of factors influencing effectiveness are presented and discussed.

Source of useful material for developing checklists, inventories etc, for assessing and developing trainers. Role types framework useful for identifying where people are and where they might need to move. Should be linked with 'Guide to Trainer Effectiveness' publication.

Buckley, R. and Caple, J., 'The Training Audit', *Journal of European Industrial Training*, 1984, vol. 8, no. 7, pp. 3–8.

Based on work done in major bank, discusses role of auditor and describes seven-stage training audit approach. Plenty of practical material and tables.

Corfield, K. Edmonstone, J. and Linacre, C., 'New Consultancy Roles for Trainers', *Leadership and Organization Development Journal*, 1984, vol. 5, no. 4, pp. 13–16.

Case study showing need for trainers to move towards developing expertise in learning design and consultancy/advisory work, as well as being an example of inter-organizational collaboration between trainers. Potential trainer roles framework – training administration, direct training, learning design, consultancy/advisory work.

Davies, J., 'Patterns and Paradoxes of Trainers' Careers – The Implications for the Influence of Training', *Journal of European Industrial Training Monograph,* 1985, vol. 9, no. 2, MCB, Bradford.

Based on research funded by the MSC. It looks at issues of trainer careers and how these relate to the organizational context trainers serve. Contents cover: career paths, trainer development, paradoxical nature of trainers' careers and development implications for link between training and organization, management issues in trainer career development, with some case studies.

Dyke, C. and Saner, M., 'Training Intervention Strategies', *Training and Development,* May 1985, pp. 10.

Describes practical experience of helping experienced trainers to learn new skills and insights. Picks up Jones' three criteria of 'getting it right', 'doing it well', and 'making it stick',

Forsyth, P. (ed.), *Managing Sales and Marketing Training,* Gower, Aldershot, 1984.

Contributed chapters covering the key elements. Four parts: (1) training for business results (the marketing context, assessing training needs, evaluating sales training); (2) developing the skills of modern marketing (basic skills, behavioural dimension, major customer dilemma, training in finance and negotiation, challenge of IT, training across national boundaries); (3) training tools and techniques (top management workshops, project-based training, programmed learning, packaged solutions, future use of video, use of training films); and (4) the organization of training (sourcing and resourcing, role of the training manager and marketing training – a new export industry). Two appendices – one a case on training in action, the other a selection from the National Training Index. Chapter 17 (the role of the training manager) has a useful section on principle functions of the T & D manager, geared to sales training.

Frank, E. and Margerison, C., 'Training Methods and Organisation Development', *Journal of European Industrial Training Monograph,* MCB, Bradford, 1978, vol. 2, no. 4.

Considers relationship between training interventions and OD, looks at applications and discusses Action Research and Action Learning. Section I covers perceptions of OD; transfer of learning problems; techniques and methods of OD and need for accurate diagnosis. Part II looks at applications under five headings – personal understanding and interpersonal skills; group problem solving and team development; group leadership and decision making; intergroup relationships; organization planning and communications. Part III is a brief discussion of Action Research and Action Learning. Part II – 50 per cent of the mongraph – useful for those wishing to learn about some intervention techniques.

Honey, P. and Mumford, A., *The Manual of Learning Styles,* Peter Honey, 1982.

Describes influences on effective learning, presents a learning style questionnaire, and discusses how this can be used for development purposes. Styles are characterized as 'activist', 'reflector', 'pragmatist', and 'theorist'.

Huczynski, A., *Encyclopedia of Management Development Methods,* Gower, pp. 339. 1983.

There must be many management trainers, developers and educators who have often wondered if no one else was going to produce a reasonable source of information and descriptions concerning management development methods. This book seems to be what they have been looking for. It is an anatomy of management development methods. The main part includes a directory of more than 300 entries, each one containing a description of the method, references to more detailed reading and cross references to complementary or related entries.

Huczynski. A., 'Training Designs for Organisational Change', *Journal of European Industrial Training.* 1983, vol. 7, no. 3, pp. 24–27.

Looks at trainers' role in helping bring about change, presents a framework for guiding training design decisions (who is the recipient of change, what is the level of the expected change, what are the relationships involved in the change), discusses how to choose training methods, and draws conclusions for trainers concerned with encouraging organizational change through training interventions.

Jones, J.A.G., 'Training Intervention Strategies', *Training and Development,* February 1985, pp. 10–12.

Argues that training effectiveness depends on how well training matches the organization, that there are three parts to effective training (getting it right, doing it well, making it stick), puts forward basic principles (process not an event, learner involvement, and contracting), and states that some new roles and skills are required.

Laird, D., *Approaches to Training and Development,* Addison-Wesley, Reading, Mass., 1978.

Helpful book, with each chapter based on a critical question. Questions are: why have a T & D department?; what do T & D officers do?; where is the T & D department located?; how do you find training needs?; how do you respond to individual training needs?; what do you do when you don't give training?; learning objectives – who needs them?; how do people learn?; what methods shall we use?; how important is teaching technique?; what should training rooms be like?; what about visual aids?; what's special about T & D budgets?; how can we measure T & D?; how do you evaluate T & D?; how do you select and care for T & D staff?; where does it all end?

Good book. Helpful charts, diagrams, and tables. Chapter 3 – on roles – contain useful material on what the roles contain and the skills needed (good for checklist development).

Law, C. and Caple, T., 'Developing the Part-time Training Manager', *Training and Development,* June 1985, pp. 24–26.

Discusses ITRU study for AnCO to create different strategy and delivery system. Describes approach taken, the needs to be met, the development strategy, the programme, use of materials and the results.

Leduchowicz, T., 'Trainer Role and Effectiveness – A Review of the Literature', *International Journal of Manpower,* 1982, vol. 3, no. 1.

Major review of contributions to looking at trainer roles and effectiveness. Summarizes key literature and present model of factors infuencing effectiveness.

Leduchowicz, T., *Guide to Trainer Effectiveness,* Manpower Services Commission/Institute of Training and Development, UK, 1984.

Based on MSC-funded research, comprises six sections: (1) what is trainer effectiveness?; (2) what do trainers do?; (3) what should be the role of the trainer?; (4) what determines trainer effectiveness?; (5) how can trainer effectiveness be assessed and (6) how can trainer effectiveness be developed?

Each section (or module) contains an exercise that can be worked through by the individual reader, in workbook fashion. Further reading and information sources provided. Good source of material and ideas for assessing and developing trainer effectiveness.

Loughary, J., and Hobson, B., *Producing Workshop Seminars and Short Courses – A Trainer's Handbook,* Association Press, Follat Publishing Company, Chicago, 812149, 1979.

This book is for anybody concerned with the design, development, running and evaluation of workshops, seminars and short courses – that is, short-term training programmes. It provides a basic model for training programmes that are one hour to four weeks in length, and illustrates how the model can be used in a variety of different situations. This model comprises five phases of contracting, designing, developing, conducting and evaluating. These are examined in detail with examples. There are nine chapters, each of which is well structured and presented with several trainer tips. They cover the nature of short-term training, solving problems through training, short-term training model, contract building, designing the course, the development stage, conducting the programme, evaluation and resources. There is a glossary and a useful index. The list of contents is very detailed and provides an excellent guide to the content of the book. Although published in America it is available through Gower Publishing.

Margerison, C., *Influencing Organisational Change – The Role of the Personnel Specialist,* IPM, London, 1978.

Two parts: (1) personal advisory skills and (2) organizational context of advisory work. Part 1 covers: what is a Personnel & OD Adviser?; personnel and OD work; what is your approach to advisory work?; establishing effective advisory discussions; cues, clues and responses; diagnosis or seduction; exploring the client's world, and a framework for advisory action. Part 2 covers: conflict and co-operation; what theories help us see; the politics of advisory work; areas for advisory action; how to identify your advisory power, and basic questions for all advisers. A very helpful book. Good checklists and instruments (e.g. the Management Adviser Situation Index, the Role Pressure Assessment Index, the Power and Influence Index, the Client Adviser Perception Index), diagrams and examples. Useful material in its own right for training managers, consultants, and advisers, and a good source of ideas.

McLagan, P.A., *Models for Excellence,* American Society for Training and Development, Washington, 1983.

Conclusions and recommendations of ASTD's Training and Development Competency Study. Describes why study needed, assumptions, methodology, study products (i.e. findings), recommendations, plus details in appendices.

'Products' cover: the HR wheel (diagram showing T & D & other HR areas); definition of T & D; future forces affecting T & D; T & D roles; critical outputs for T & D function; competency model for T & D; role profiles, role clusters and profiles; roles/competencies matrix (showing which roles contain which competencies). Some 80 pages devoted to products. 15 key roles identified, including the manager of T & D.

Excellent material for building checklists, workbooks, assessment instruments. Good, detailed descriptions, especially the Competency model with its examples of behaviour illustrating levels of expertise.

Pepper, A.C., *Managing the Training and Development Function,* Gower, Aldershot, 1984.

Based on view that T & D needs to be managed with at least as much care as any other function. Draws on authors 30 years of experience.

Two parts. Part I, about management of training, has 15 chapters covering definitions, policies and practices, intentions and objectives, training opportunities/matrix, notifiable and non-notifiable training, an agent of change, implementation and change, evaluation of training, costs and benefits plus CB analysis, use of objectives, offering a service, and training officers.

Part II is about managing manpower development and has 14 chapters on training and manpower development, planning, economic and political context, planning and the individual, philosophies of development, conflicts, managers, career development, managing career development and auditing the T & D function. Case histories used illustrating analysis, planning, decision making and action.

Useful bibliography covering 13 areas (e.g. T & D Function, Board's Responsibilities, Organization Design and Development Employee as a Learner, etc.) plus publishers' details. Not all entries annotated – most are.

Pettigrew, A.M., Jones, G.R., and Reason, P.W., *Training and Development Roles in their Organisational Setting,* Manpower Services Commission, 1982.

Describes findings of study, of the role of the training officer in the UK chemical industry. Though limited to one industry, concepts apply elsewhere.

Seven parts: Part 1 describes objectives, method and sample of phase 1 of research; part 2 provides five perspectives on the TO role; part 3 looks at boundary management and the TO role; part 4 describes phase 2 research; part 5 looks at the TO in his role set; part 6 describes workshops for reviewing TO roles, while part 7 offers conclusions and recommendations. Limited references and readings are provided.

Rae, L., *The Skills of Training – A Guide for Managers and Practitioners,* Gower, 1983, pp. 181.

Introductory book, aimed to fill the gap between the slim glossaries of training terms and the lengthy volumes covering individual techniques. It reviews the main techniques, methods and approaches currently used in training and development. Each of these are described briefly with advantages and disadvantages set out and also an indication of the most appropriate use of the technique or method. Written for someone newly appointed to a training job and will appeal to line managers who have an interest in or responsibility for the training and development of their own staff.

Robinson, K.R., *A Handbook of Training Management* (2nd edn.), Kogan Page, London, 1985.

Useful book covering: the development of the training profession; training objectives, policies and strategies; establishing training needs; planning the overall programme; learning and behaviour; methods and techniques of training; measuring and following-up results; training resources; influences on the training function, and review and possible trends. Very little on roles or how to change them.

Schein, E., *Process Consultation – Its Role in OD* Addison-Wesley, Reading, Mass., 1969.

Although dated, this is a good source of knowledge, ideas and practice about diagnosis and intervention in organizations. Two parts: (1) diagnosis – about process consultation; overview of human processes in organizations; communication processes; functional roles of group members; group problem-solving and decision-making; group norms and group growth; leadership and authority; intergroup processes: (2) intervention – establishing contact and defining a relationship; selecting a setting and a method of work; gathering data; intervention; evaluation of results and disengagement. Although mainly aimed at consultants and OD specialists/students, contains material of use to trainers operating consulting, advisory, change agent type roles.

Scriven, R., 'Learning Circles', *Journal of European Industrial Training,* 1984, vol. 8, no. 1, pp. 17–20.

Describes model for changing the emphasis of training in Shell International from teaching focus to encouraging learning. Problems and benefits discussed. Method gets training back to the job, and the manager away from the classroom. T & D provides backup support, help, guidance etc (e.g. training boss to be mentor, developing distance learning materials).

Taylor, B., and Lippitt, G., (eds.), *Management Development and Training Handbook,* McGraw-Hill, 1983.

This is the second edition of this handbook, which was well received the first time round (to the extent of now being claimed a 'classic'). This edition is new, revised and updated. It has 18 new chapters dealing with new research and key areas of management development in the 1980s; 13 chapters have been revised and updated; and two 'classic' chapters from the original have been retained. To some extent it is more a new handbook than a revised edition.

Several of the chapters will be helpful to trainers and managers of training e.g. the role of the central management development service (Chapter 8) organizational diagnosis (Chapter 9), the use of attitude surveys (Chapter 13). All will be of interest.

Structured in four parts: management development and training scene, management development and training system, management development and training methods, and management development and training programmes.

Thakur, M., Bristow, J., and Carby, K. (eds.), *Personnel in Change – OD Through the Personnel Function,* IPM, London, 1978.

Useful view, with cases and examples, of OD and the role personnel can play, in managing change. Covers: introduction to OD; role of personnel in a changing environment; introduction of OD to the practice of personnel (with a section on training); case studies in OD. The section on training has some useful principles of a developmental approach to training, with examples.

Varney, C.H., *O.D. for Managers,* Addison-Wesley, Reading, Mass., 1977.

Excellent book. Practical, readable, full of ideas, guide-notes, etc. Very good for trainers as well as managers involved with change. Covers: changing environment and OD; what is OD?; planned organizational change; steps in the OD process; factors affecting need for change; ways to collect organizational information; planning, initiating and measuring organizational change; OD techniques; building an effective management team; installing an OD programme. Checklists, diagrams, cases, action-steps etc.

Wright, P., 'Training Budgets – Are They Obsolete?', *Journal of European Industrial Training,* 1984, vol. 8, no. 7, pp. 22–24.

Should organizations look to 'performers' or 'performance' when seeking improvements? Argues that most improvements can be found in work situation. Asks if training is justified.

Zenger, J. *Training for Organisational Excellence,* Paper presented to 'STADA' Conference, January 1985 (Singapore).

Draws on extensive experience of Zenger Miller consultants. Proposes that the best ones (i.e. training functions) have 10 factors in common: clear vision of goal and mission of training; tightly linked to organization's objectives, line management commitment and involvement, excellent management practice within the training function, emphasis on practicality, use multiple sources, consistent delivery, sense of urgency, achieve critical mass, evaluation of results.
    Excellent paper with good material.
    Reprinted in *JEIT* 1985, vol. 9, no. 7, pp. 3–8.

Bibliography

Argyris, C. (1970): *Intervention Theory and Method:* Addison-Wesley, Reading, Mass.

Baird, J.E. (1980): 'Enhancing Managerial Credibility': *Personnel Journal.*

Bandura, A. (1977): *Social Learning Theory:* Prentice-Hall, Inc., Engelwood Cliffs, New Jersey.

Bennett, R. (1983): 'The Effective Trainer': *Training and Development,* August.

Bennett, R. (1985): 'How to Survive as a Trainer': *Journal of European Industrial Training,* vol. 9, no. 6.

Bennett, R. (1986): *Adopting the Right Role (Workbook):* Trainer Support Services.

Bennett, R., and Laidlaw, W. (1986): *Managing the Business of Training (Workbook):* Trainer Support Services.

Bennett, R., and Leduchowicz, T. (1982): *A Report on the Trainer Effectiveness Project:* Thames Valley Regional Management Centre.

Bennett, R., and Leduchowicz, T. (1983): What Makes for an Effective Trainer?: *Journal of European Industrial Training Monograph,* vol. 7, no. 2.

Bigge, M.L. (1982): *Learning Theories for Teachers:* Harper & Row, New York.

Binsted, D. (1986): *Developments in Interpersonal Skills Training:* Gower.

Bowen, P. (1976): *Social Control in Industrial Organisations:* Routledge and Kegan Paul, London.

Bruner, J.S. (1960): *The Process of Education:* Harvard University Press.

Bruner, J.S. (1966): *Toward a Theory of Instruction:* Belknap.

Burdett, J. (1985): 'Building a Values Driven Culture': *The Human Resource,* Oct/Nov.

Camp, R.R. et al. (1986): *Toward a More Effective Training Strategy and Practice:* Prentice-Hall, Inc., Engelwood Cliffs, New Jersey.

Campbell, A. (1984): 'Knowing "culture" of a firm is vital': *The Globe and Mail:* Monday June 25th.

Churchill, G.A. et al. (1985): 'The Determinants of Salesperson Performance – A Meta-analysis': *Journal of Marketing Research,* vol. 12, May, pp. 103–118.

Corwin, R. (1972): 'Strategies for Organisational Intervention – An Empirical Comparison': *American Sociological Review:* August, pp. 441–442.

Craig, R.L. (ed.) (1976): *Training and Development Handbook:* 2nd edn. McGraw-Hill.

Davis, H.L., and Silk, A.J. (1972): 'Interaction and Influence Processes in Personal Selling': *Sloan Management Review,* vol. 13, no. 2, pp. 59–76.

Davies, J. (1985): 'Patterns and Paradoxes of Trainers' Careers – The Implications for the Influence of Training': *Journal of European Industrial Training Monograph,* vol. 9, no. 2.

Davies, J. and Burgoyne, J. (1984): *Career Paths of Direct Trainers:* Manpower Services Commission, UK.

Drake, M.A. (1984): 'Information and Corporate Cultures': *Special Libraries,* October, p. 263.

Eitington, J.E. (1984): *The Winning Trainer:* Gulf Houston.

Field, L.M. and Davies, A. (1984): 'Corporate Culture and Corporate Success': *The Canadian Manager,* June, p. 5.

(The) Financial Post (1983): Companies' Workers Voice Concerns about VDTs: Nov. 5th, p. 51.

Flegg, D.W. (1983): 'Developing Instructors to Meet Training Needs': *Personnel Management,* May.

Foo Meng Tong (1985): 'Roles of the Trainer': *STADA Annual,* Singapore Training and Development Association.

French, W.L. and Bell, C.H. (1973): *Organisational Development:* Prentice-Hall, Inc., Engelwood Cliffs, New Jersey.

French, J.R.P. and Raven, B.H. (1959): 'The bases of social power' in D. Cartwright (ed.), *Studies in Social Power,* University of Michigan Press, Michigan.

Futrell, C.M. (1980): *ABC's of Selling:* Irwin.

Gill, R.W.T. (1985): *Our Training Philosophy:* Roger Gill & Associates Mission Statement.

Goldsmith, W. and Clutterbuck, D. (1984): *The Winning Streak:* Weidenfeld & Nicolson, London.

Hagedorn, H.J. (1984): 'Everybody into the Pool': *Across the Board:* October, p. 26.

Handy, C. (1976): *Understanding Organizations:* 1st edn. Penguin, Harmondsworth.

Harris, W.J.A. (1975): 'The Distance Tutor Education by Correspondence': *Manchester Monograph* no. 3.

Hodgson, V. (1985): 'Distance Learning in Management Education': *Journal of Innovative Higher Education:* vol. 2, no. 1.

Hurst, W.C. (1981): 'Coping with Change – Use The Action Learning Approaches': *Industrial Training Service Ltd. Monograph.*

James, K. (1980): 'The development of senior managers for the future': in J. Beck and C. Cox (eds.), *Advances in Management Education:* Wiley.

Jones, J.A.G. (1981): 'Figure of Eight Evaluation – A Fundamental Change in the Trainer's Approach': *Training Officer,* Sept.

Jones, J.A.G. (1982): 'Making Trainer Interventions More Effective': *Journal of European Industrial Training,* vol. 6, no. 6.

Jones, J.A.G. (1983): 'Training Intervention Strategies – 'An Opportunity to Develop the Role of the Manager': *Training and Development,* Sept.

Kast, F. and Rosenzweig, J. (1974): *Organisation and Management – A Systems Approach:* McGraw-Hill.

Katz, R. (1982): Managing Careers – the Influence of Job and Group Longevities, in R. Katz (ed.), *Career Issues in Human Resource Management,* Prentice-Hall, Inc., Engelwood Cliffs, New Jersey.

Kipnis, D. and Schmidt, S.M. (1982): *Profiles of Organisational Influence Strategies:* University Associates, San Diego, CA.

Kolb, D.A. et al. (1979): *Organisational Psychology – An Experimental Approach:* Prentice-Hall, Inc., Engelwood Cliffs, New Jersey.

Lastra, B. and Nichols, M.B. (1978): 'Define and Broadcast Your Training Philosophy': *Training,* Nov. p. 387.

Leduchowicz, T. (1982): Trainer Role and Effectiveness – A Review of the Literature: *International Journal of Manpower,* vol. 3, no. 1, pp. 2–9.

Leduchowicz, T. (1974): *Guide to Trainer Effectiveness:* Manpower Services Commission/Institute of Training and Development.

Lyppitt, G. (1982): *Organisational Renewal:* 2nd edn., Prentice-Hall, Inc., Engelwood Cliffs, New Jersey.

Loughary, J.W. and Hepson, B. (1976): *Producing Workshops, Seminars and Short Courses – A Trainer's Handbook,* Follett Publishing Co.

McLagen, P.A. (1983): *Models for Excellence:* American Society for Training Development.

McHale, J. and Flegg, D.W. (1985): *Putting It Across – The OPTIS Guide to Effective Instruction:* OPTIS, Oxford.

McKay, L. and Torrington, D. (1986): 'Training – Down but Not Out?': *Journal of European Industrial Training,* vol. 10, no. 1.

Maier, N.F.R. (1963): *Problem Solving Discussions and Conferences:* McGraw-Hill.

Maier, N.F.R. and Verser, G. (1982): *Psychology in Industrial Organisations:* Houghton Mifflin, Boston, Mass.

Manpower Services Commission (1978): *First Report of the Training of Trainers Committee:* UK.

Manpower Services Commission (1985): *A Challenge to Complacency – Changing Attitudes to Training:* UK.

Margerison C.J. (1980): How Chief Executives Succeed: *Journal of European Industrial Training Monograph,* vol. 4, no. 5.

Margerison, C.J. (1984): 'Existential management development', in C. Cox and J. Beck (eds.), *Advances of Management Education,* Wiley.

Margerison, C.J. (1984): 'Where is management education going?' in A. Kakabadase and S. Mukhi (eds.), *The Future of Management Education,* Gower.

Margerison, C.J. and Kakabadase, A. (1984): *How American Chief Executives Succeed:* American Management Association.

Margerison, C.J. and McCann, D.J. (1984): *How to Lead a Winning Team:* MCB University Press, Bradford, West Yorkshire.

Margerison, C.J. and McCann, D.J. (1984) *The Margerison McCann Team Management Index:* MCB University Press, Bradford, West Yorkshire.

Nadler, L. (1969): 'The Variety of Training Roles': *Industrial and Commercial Training,* vol. 1, no. 1.

Nadler, L. (1982): *Designing Training Programmes:* Addison-Wesley, Reading, Mass.

Newsham, D. (1975): *What's In a Style?:* Industrial Training Research Unit, Cambridge, UK.

Otto, C.P. and Glaser, R.O. (1970): *The Management of Training:* Addison-Wesley, Reading, Mass.

Pascale, R. (1984): 'Fitting New Employees into the Corporate Culture': *Fortune,* May 28th.

Pepper, A.D. (1984): *Managing the Training and Development Function:* Gower.

Peters, T. and Waterman, R. (1982): *In Search of Excellence:* Harper & Row, New York.

Pettigrew, A. (1982): *Sharing in the Human Resource Management Task - Roles for Personnel, Trainers and Managers?:* Institute of Personnel Management, UK.

Pettigrew, A., et al. (1982): *Training and Development Roles in their Organisational Setting:* Manpower Services Commission, UK.

Pffeifer, J.W. and Jones, J. (1972): *Handbook of Structured Experiences for Human Relations Training:* University Associates, San Diego, CA.

Phillips, K. and Fraser, T. (1982): *The Management of Interpersonal Skills Training:* Gower.

Rae, L. (1983): *The Skills of Training - A Guide for Managers and Practitioners:* Gower.

Rae, L. (1985): *The Skills of Human Relations Training - A Guide for Managers and Practitioners:* Gower.

Revans, R. (1982) *The Origins and Growth of Action Learning:* Chartwell Bratt.

Robinson, K. (1985): *A Handbook of Training Management:* Kogan Page, London.

Schwind, H.F. (1985): 'The State of the Art in Cross-Cultural Management Training': *International HRD Journal,* vol. 1 Feb.

Silverfarb, H.I. (1977): 'Training Policy': *Multinational Banks Regional Training Centre Principles and Practices.*

Singer, E.J. (1977): *Training in Industry and Commerce:* Institute of Personnel Management, UK.

Skills Development Fund (1985): 'Getting the Framework Right': *Notes for Managers Series 2,* Singapore.

Skinner, B.F. (1979): *Beyond Freedom and Dignity:* Pelican Books.

Spoor, J. (1986): *Managing for Success (Workbook):* Trainer Support Services.

Thames Valley Training (1985): Journal of the Thames Valley Training Association, UK.

Ulrich, W.L. (1984): 'HRM and Culture – History, Ritual and Myth': *Human Resources Management,* Summer.

Walker, J.W. (ed.) (1979): *The Challenge of Human Resource Planning – Selected Readings:* Human Resource Planning Society.

Wills, G.S.C. (1984): *Demonstrable Productivity from Management Education:* MCB University Press, Bradford, West Yorkshire.

Wright, P. (1983): 'Strategic Planning and Human Resources Planning – the Vital Link': *Training and Development Journal:* January.

Zenger, J. (1985): 'Training for Organisational Excellence': *STADA Annual,* Singapore Training and Development Association.

Index